I0722073

The vilest deeds, like poison weeds,
bloom well in prison air.
It is only what is good in man, that wastes and withers there.
            — Oscar wilde (ballad of Reading Gaol)

Cofounders: Taj Forer and Michael Itkoff
Creative Director: Ursula Damm
Copy Editor: Gabrielle Fastman

ISBN: 978-1-954119-30-7

Printed by Ofset Yapimevi, Turkey.

Daylight Books
E-mail: info@daylightbooks.org
Web: www.daylightbooks.org

ARA OSHAGAN

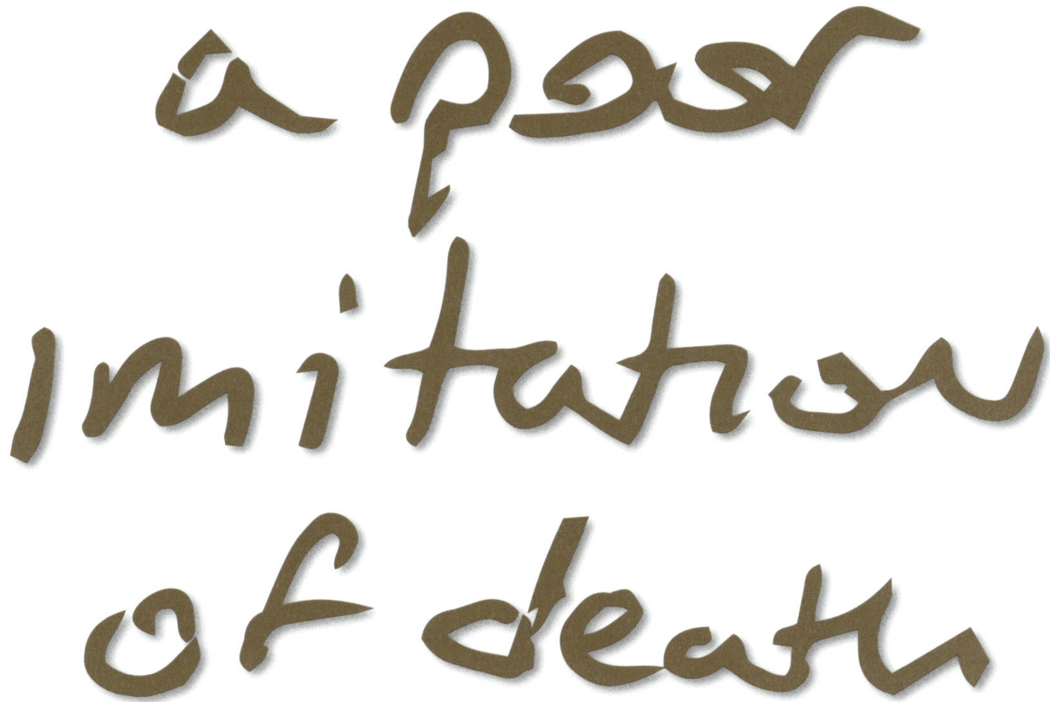

Youth in the California Prison System

Foreword by Father Gregory Boyle

Daylight

Foreword

by Father Gregory Boyle

World renowned for "radical kinship" and "boundless compassion," Father Gregory Boyle is the founder of Homeboy Industries, the largest gang reentry program in the United States and a national model. He is the author of three books, including the 2010 *New York Times* bestseller *Tattoos on the Heart: The Power of Boundless Compassion*.

"Throw away the key." Human beings have always liked that expression. We feel good about ourselves afterwards. We think it clear-eyed, tough, and believe it sends the right message: we mean business.

Countless are the number of kids I know who sit in cells where the key has been thrown away. The United States remains the only country on earth that sentences children to die in prison. It is hard, sometimes, to get out from under that shame.

There is an idea that's taken root in the world and it is at the root of all that's wrong with it. And that idea would be this: that there just might be lives out there that matter less than other lives. *A Poor Imitation of Death* stands against that idea. With powerful photographs and poignant texts from kids themselves, this book stands with the demonized so that the demonizing will stop. It stands with the "disposable" so that the day will come when we stop throwing kids away.

The late, great child psychologist Alice Miller calls on us all to be "enlightened witnesses": people who through our kindness and tenderness and focused, attentive love "return kids to themselves." With children, you don't hold the bar up and ask them to measure up, you just show up and hold the mirror up. Then you tell them the truth: that they are exactly what God had in mind when God made them. Then you watch them become that truth; inhabit that truth. And no bullet can pierce it, no four prison walls can keep it out, and death can't touch it, because it is that huge.

The book you hold in your hands is an enlightened witness. It points us to the culturally disparaged and asks us to stand in awe at what these kids have to carry, rather than in judgment at how they carry it. Each photograph invites us into a mutuality with the subjects here presented and proposes kinship with them. For, in the end, the measure of our compassion lies not in our service to these kids but in our willingness to see ourselves in kinship with them.

We are invited, through this fine book, to stand with the easily despised and the readily left out. And you can almost hear those who would have us throw away the key accuse our solidarity with such kids as a waste of our time. But the prophet Jeremiah writes, "In this place of which you say, it is a waste … there will be heard again, the voice of mirth and the voice of gladness … the voices of those who sing."

A Poor Imitation of Death makes those voices heard.

I Am Human

by Ara Oshagan

When the handcuffs are placed on Duc, he is most worried about his dad. Brutal visions are floating in his mind: fierce beating, extension-cord whipping, screaming, blood. Duc is not worried about the handcuffs. He is worried about what his dad might do to him when he gets out.

Duc is sixteen years old. He is the son of Vietnamese working-class immigrants. His dad is often unemployed and home life is unstable and sometimes violent. When not racked by depression, Duc does well in school. But sometimes he gets into fights and is sent home. There, he must face his dad's wrath. He attempts running away from home, suicide even. Psychological evaluations, however, stress the likelihood of Duc outgrowing his problems.

Duc and two buddies are cruising down a back alley looking for a car and a fight. Duc is driving. They find the car and approach. Suddenly, gunfire from the back seat explodes in his ear. He bolts, loses control of his car, and slams into the other car. His ears are ringing. He jams his car into reverse and flees. No one in either car is hurt.

It is Duc's first offense. He is held at Los Angeles Central Juvenile Hall but tried as an adult. The initial charge is assault with a deadly weapon. Then first-degree attempted murder, though no gunshot residue is found nor any of Duc's prints on the gun. Then gang enhancements are added and he is charged with thirty-five years to life. Duc now starts to worry about the handcuffs.

A twenty-seven-year deal is on the table. Tried as an adult, he can't talk to his parents, who sit within sight in the courtroom. From a payphone in his holding cell, he calls one of his instructors from juvenile hall. What should he do? Accept to go to prison for twenty-seven years? Wait for another offer? Go to trial? Duc is seventeen years old.

When convicted on all counts and sentenced to thirty-five years to life, he is no longer worried about his dad at all. He won't even be up for parole until 2031, when he is forty-eight years old and his dad a frail old man—if still alive. His mind is an empty vessel. He is floating away.

Duc arrives at Tehachapi—a Level IV super-maximum-security state prison. It is 1:00 a.m. It is pitch black. Cages are rattling and everyone is screaming. Chaos. He is told to wait, his only possessions—sheets and a blanket—in his arms. It is so loud he can't hear himself think. He is the smallest person in the world. He is not Duc anymore. He doesn't know who he is.

He thinks, I am human just like everyone else. I like to read. I like to write. I want people to love me for me. To sit down with me and just get to know me and talk to me. I'm not a lost cause ...

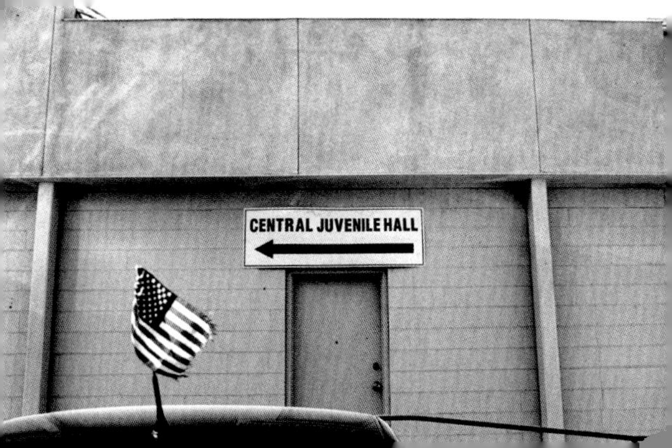
CENTRAL JUVENILE HALL

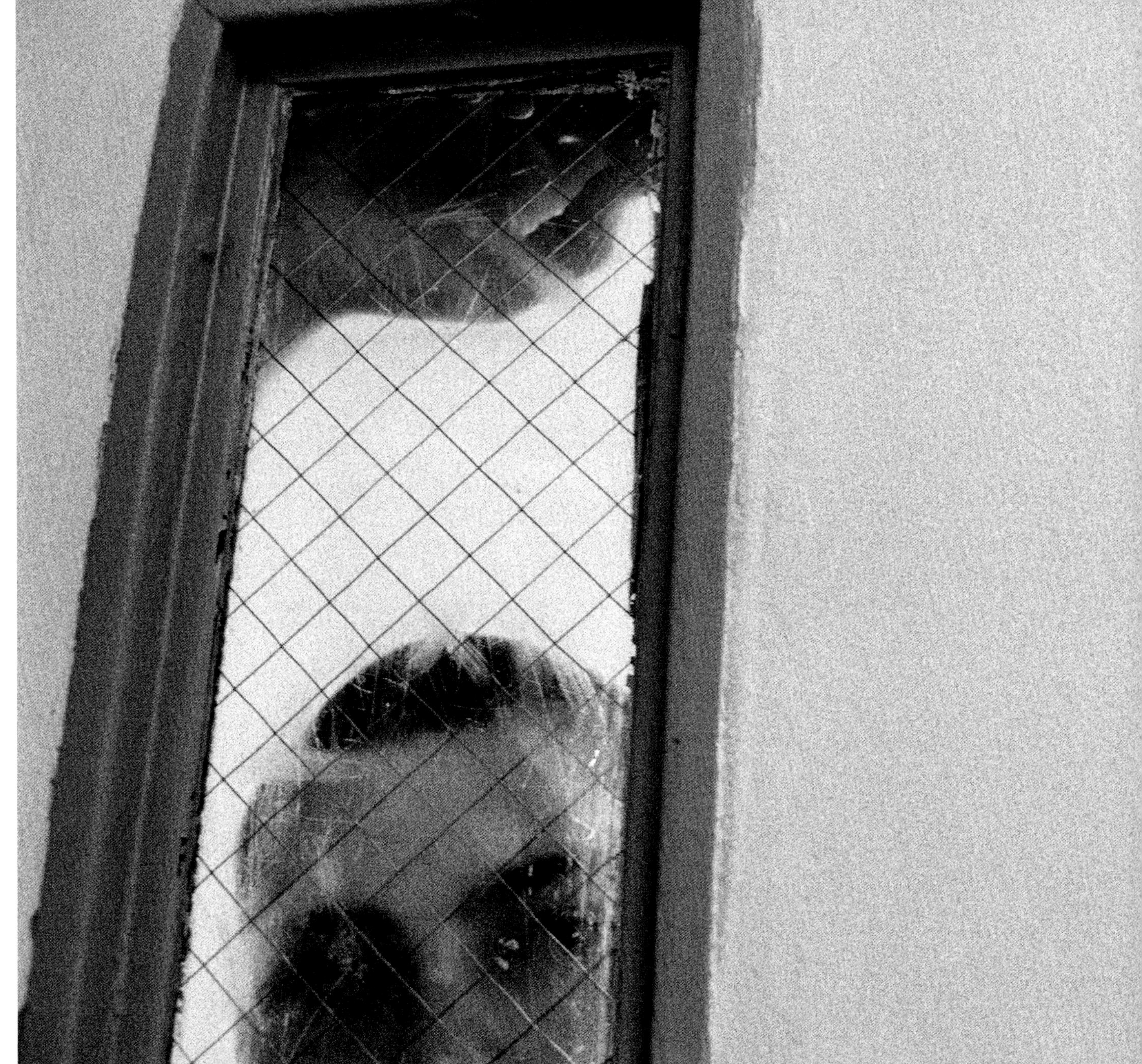

Every year, nearly half a
million youth under the age
of eighteen are arrested.

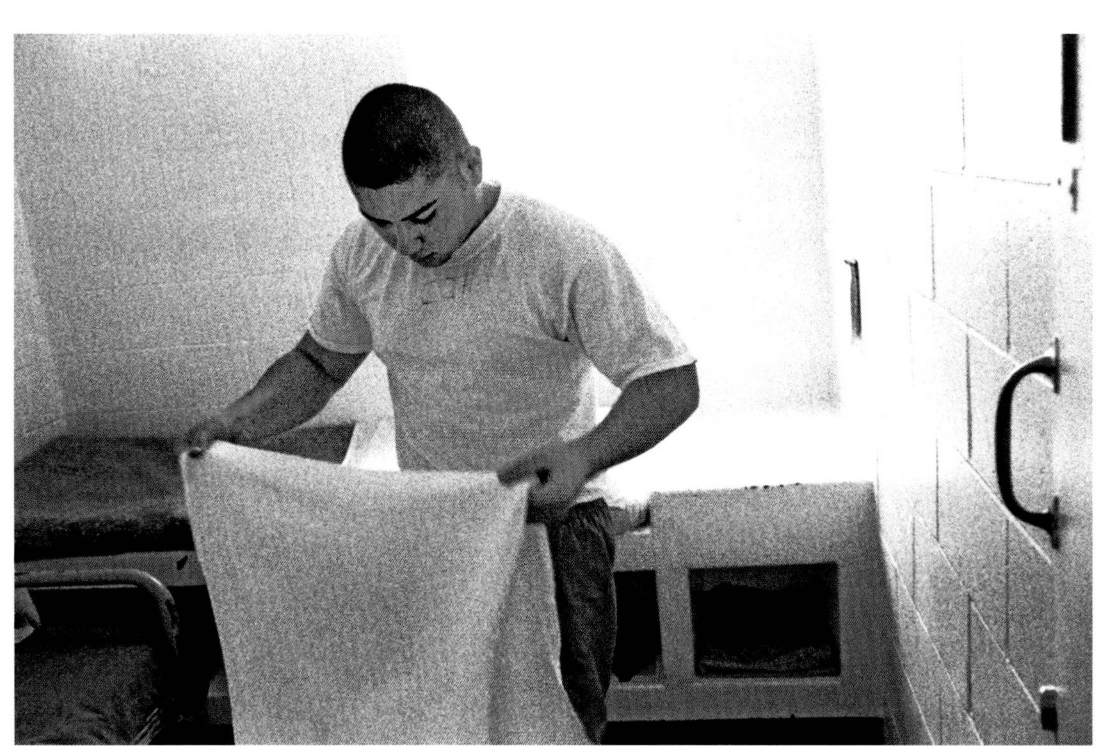

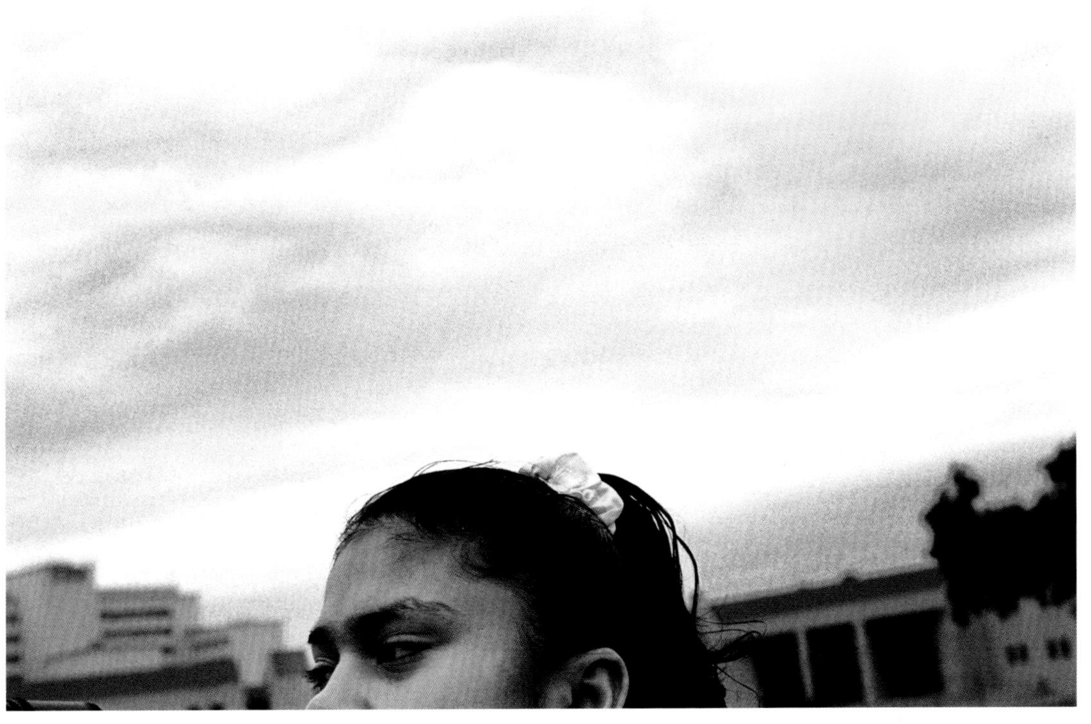

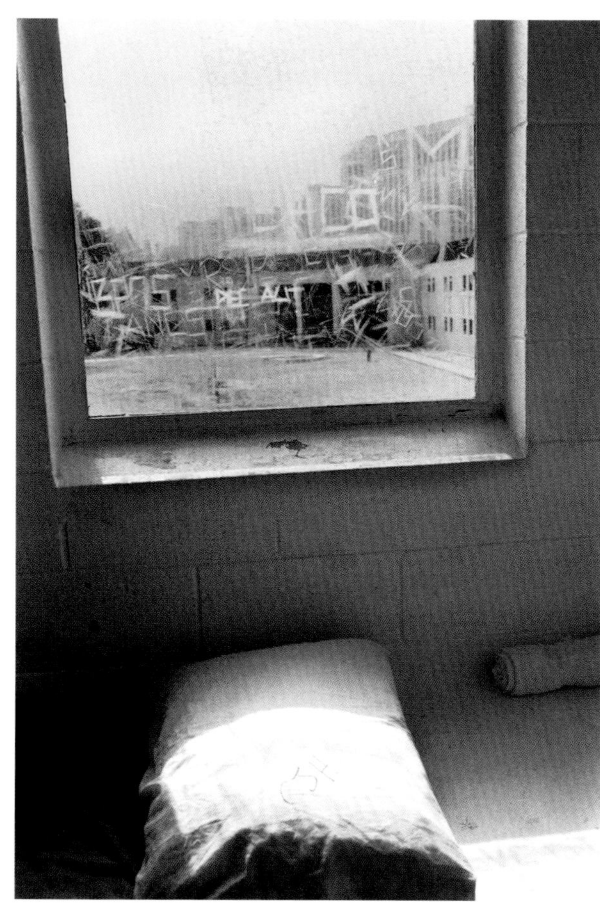

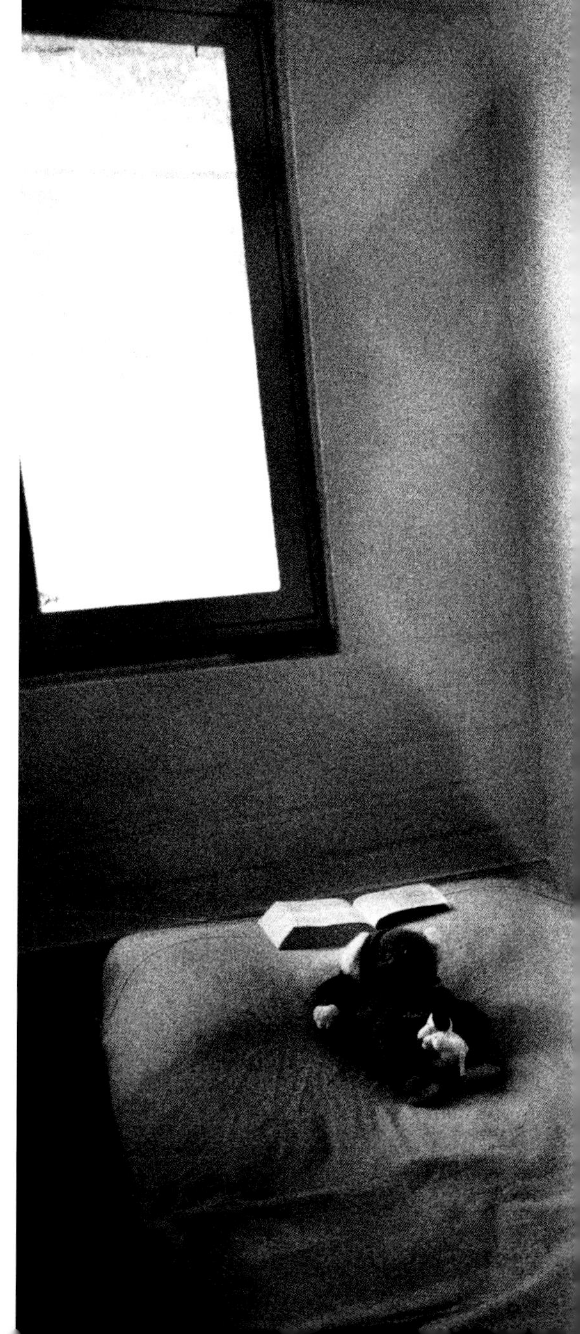

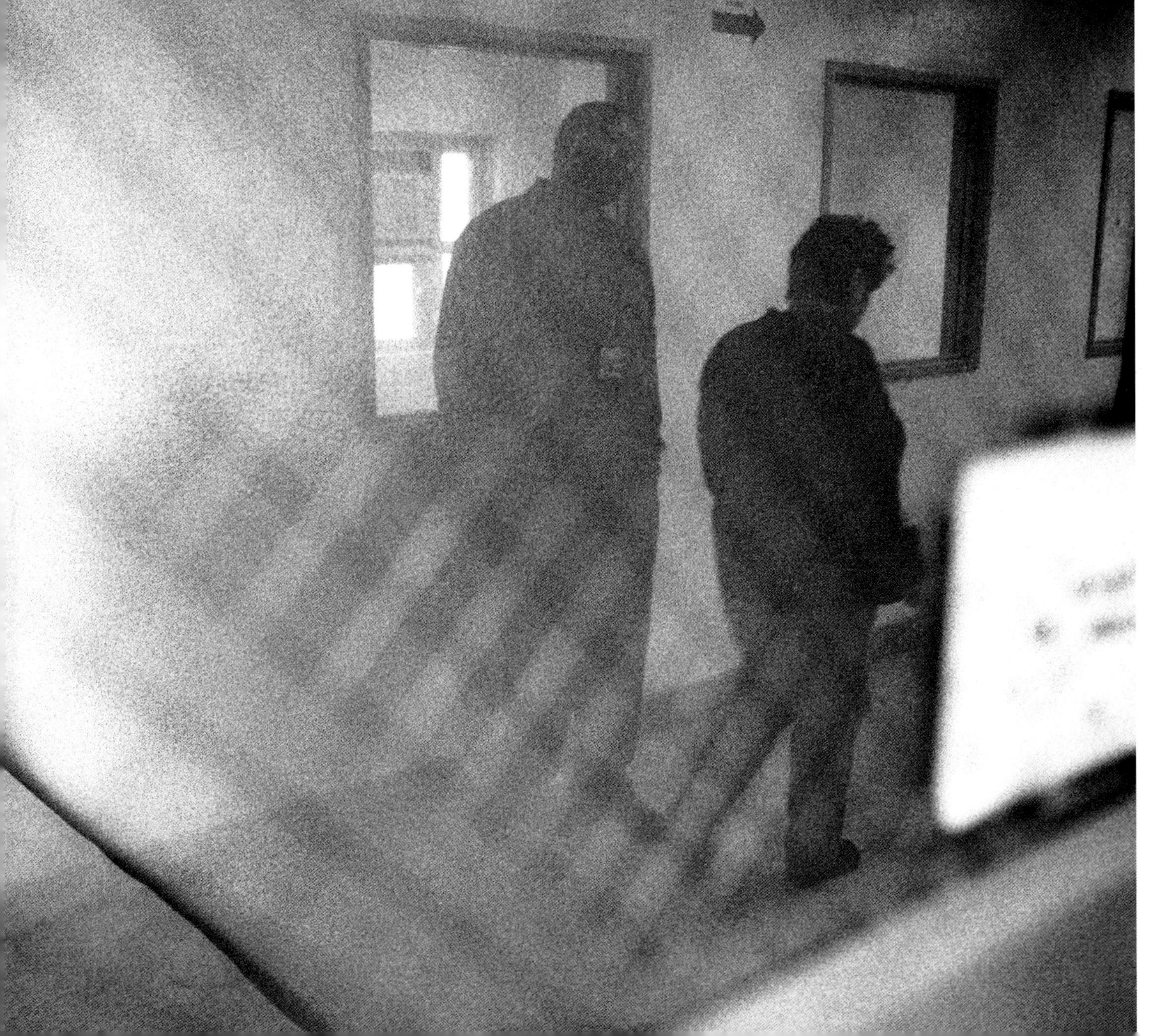

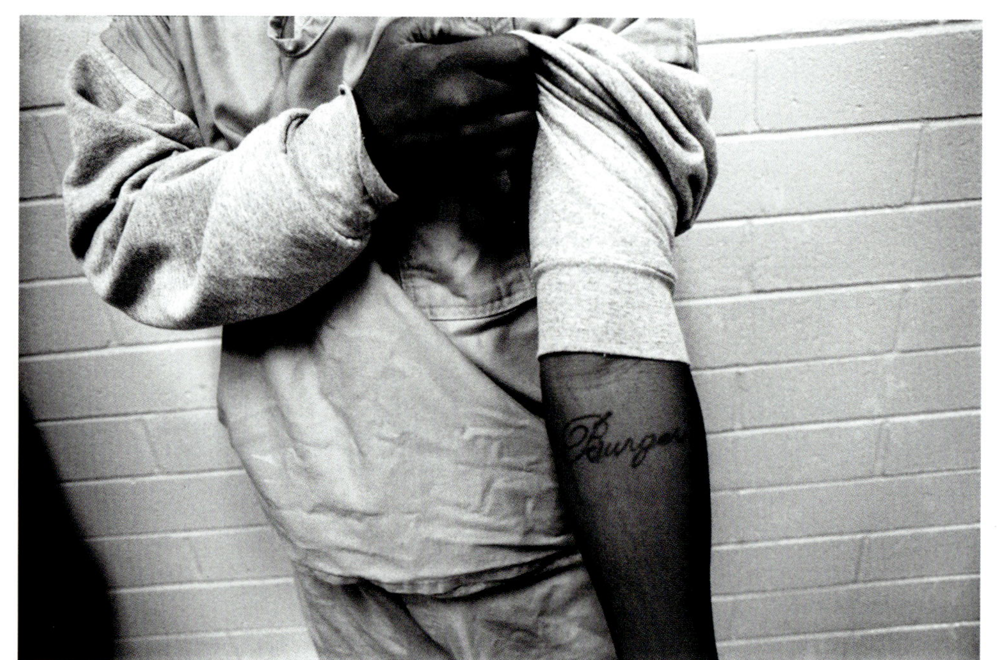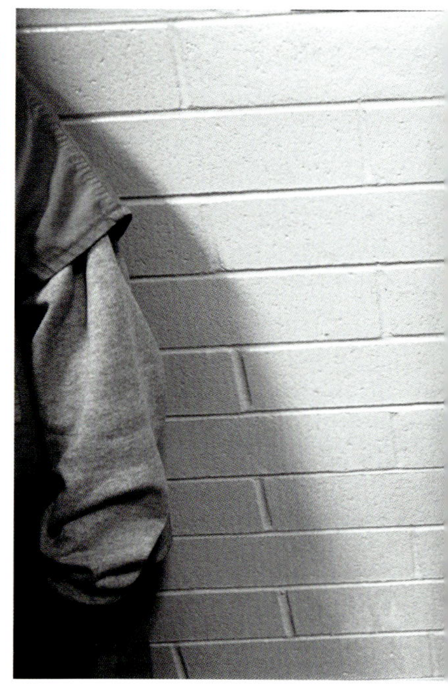

I love my
it will B

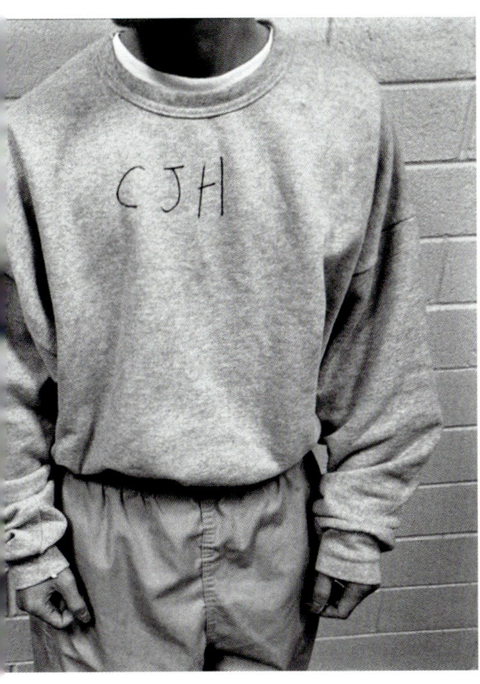 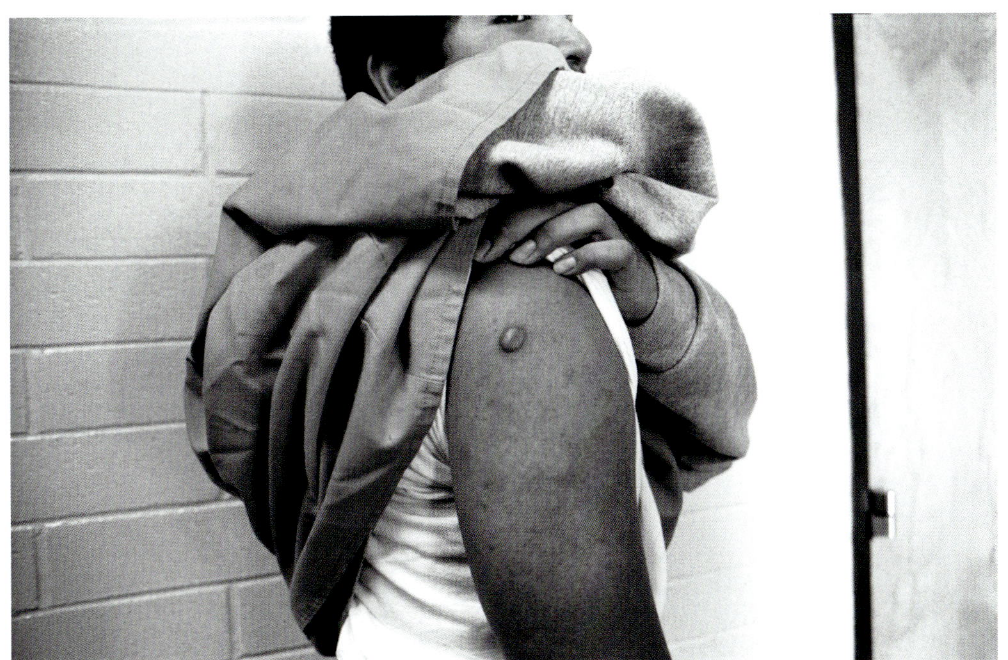

narrjo to death But for I knew
the peath of me

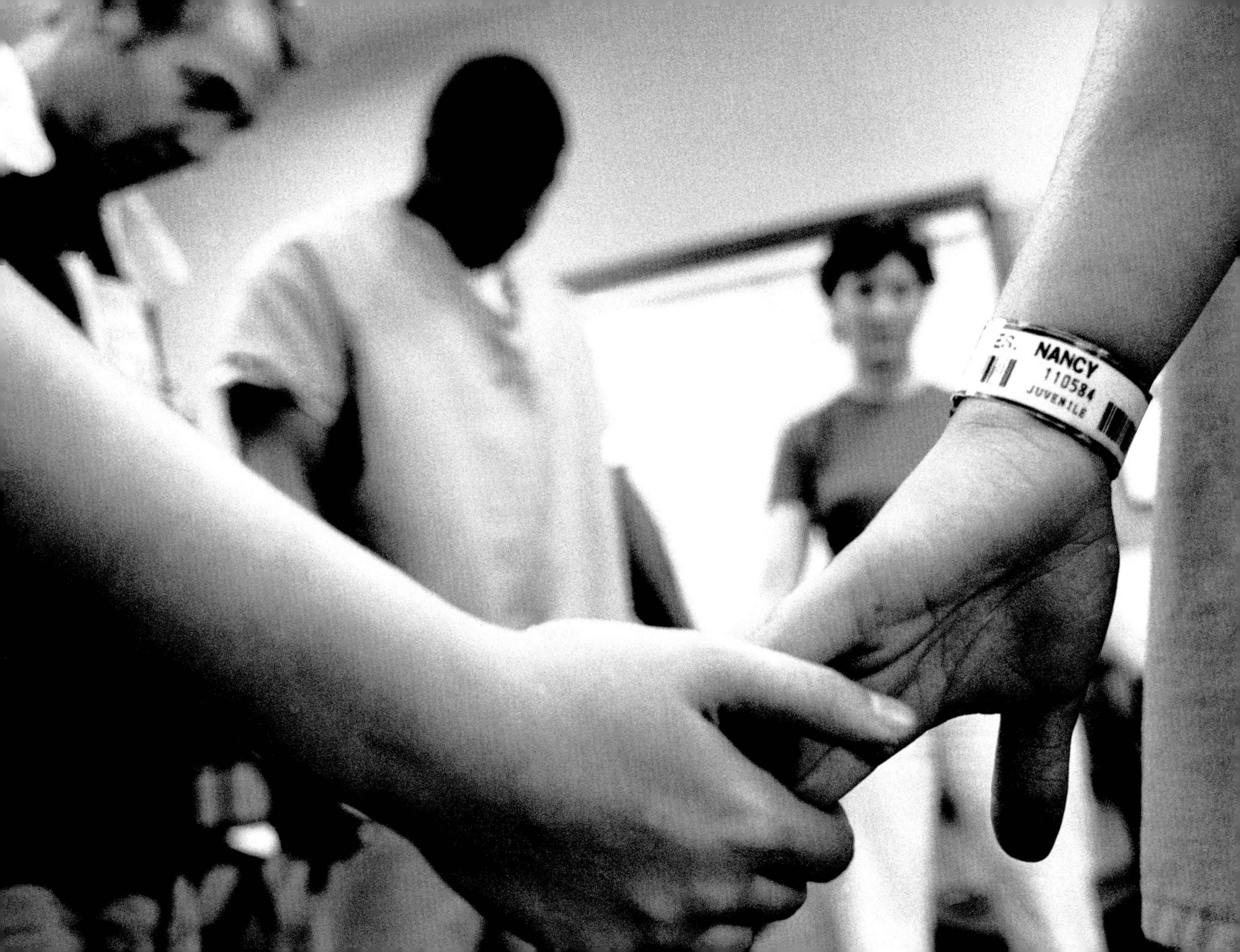
ES.
NANCY
110584
JUVENILE

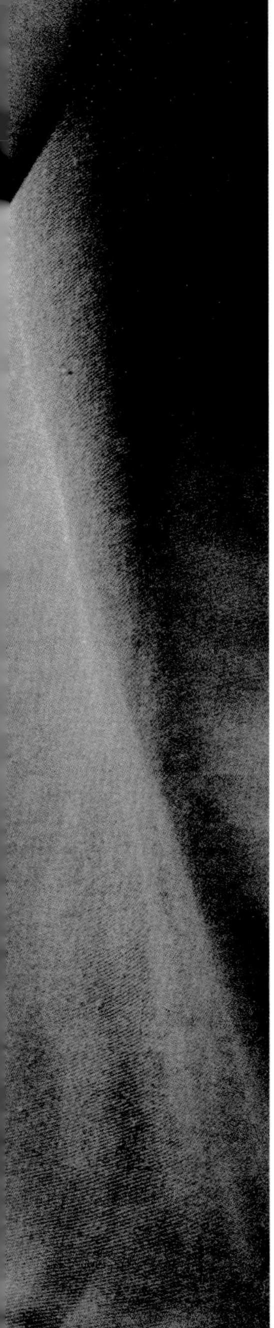

More than 200,000 youth
are tried, sentenced, or
incarcerated as adults
every year.

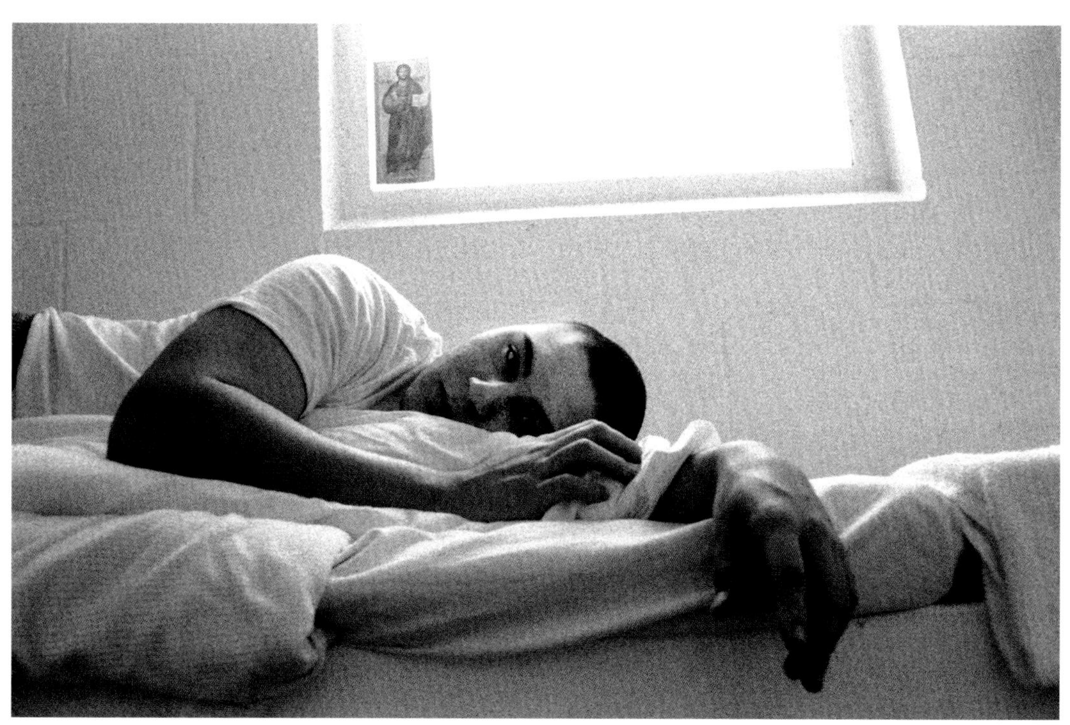

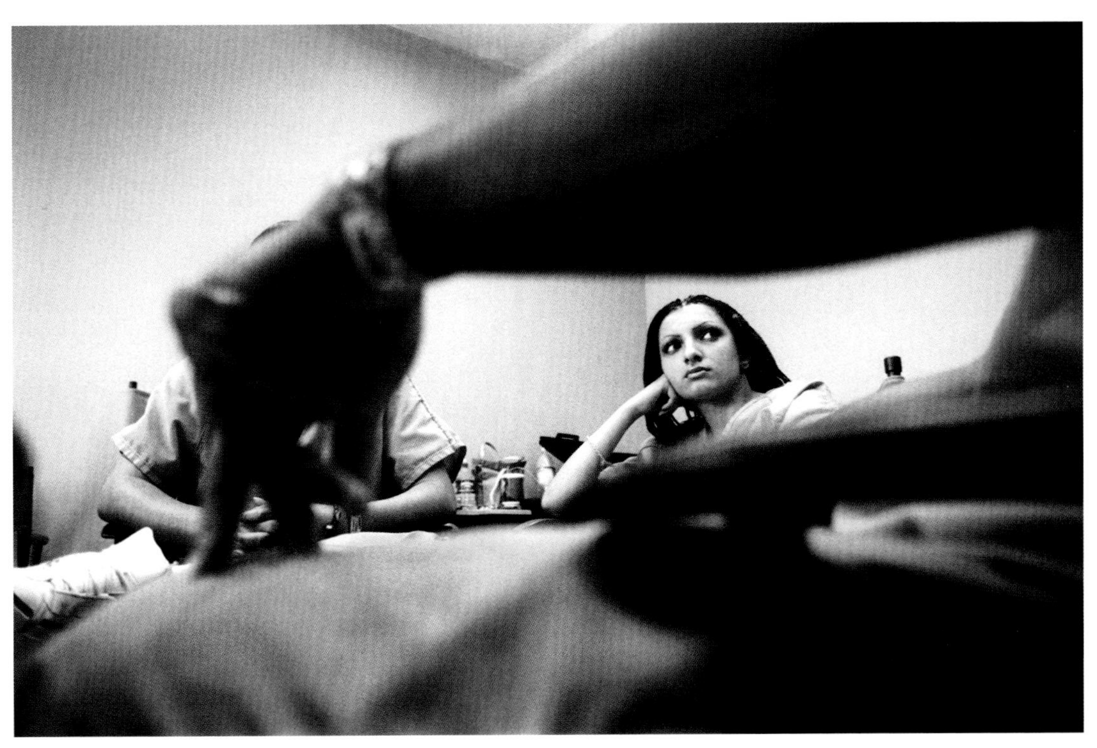

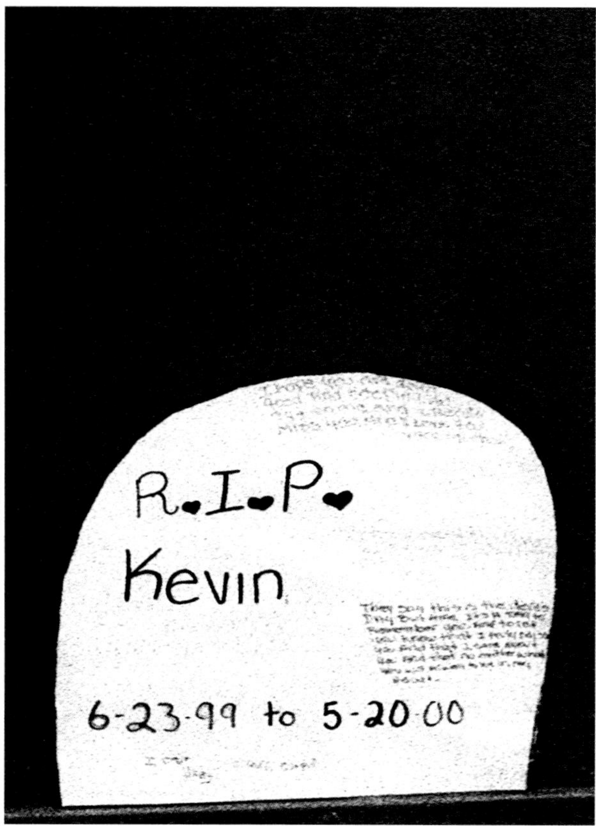

Nancy's one-and-a-half-year-old baby boy, Kevin, drowned in an accident and she was charged with second-degree attempted murder for his death on inconclusive evidence. Nancy was sixteen years old at the time and was sentenced to seven years. It was her first offense.

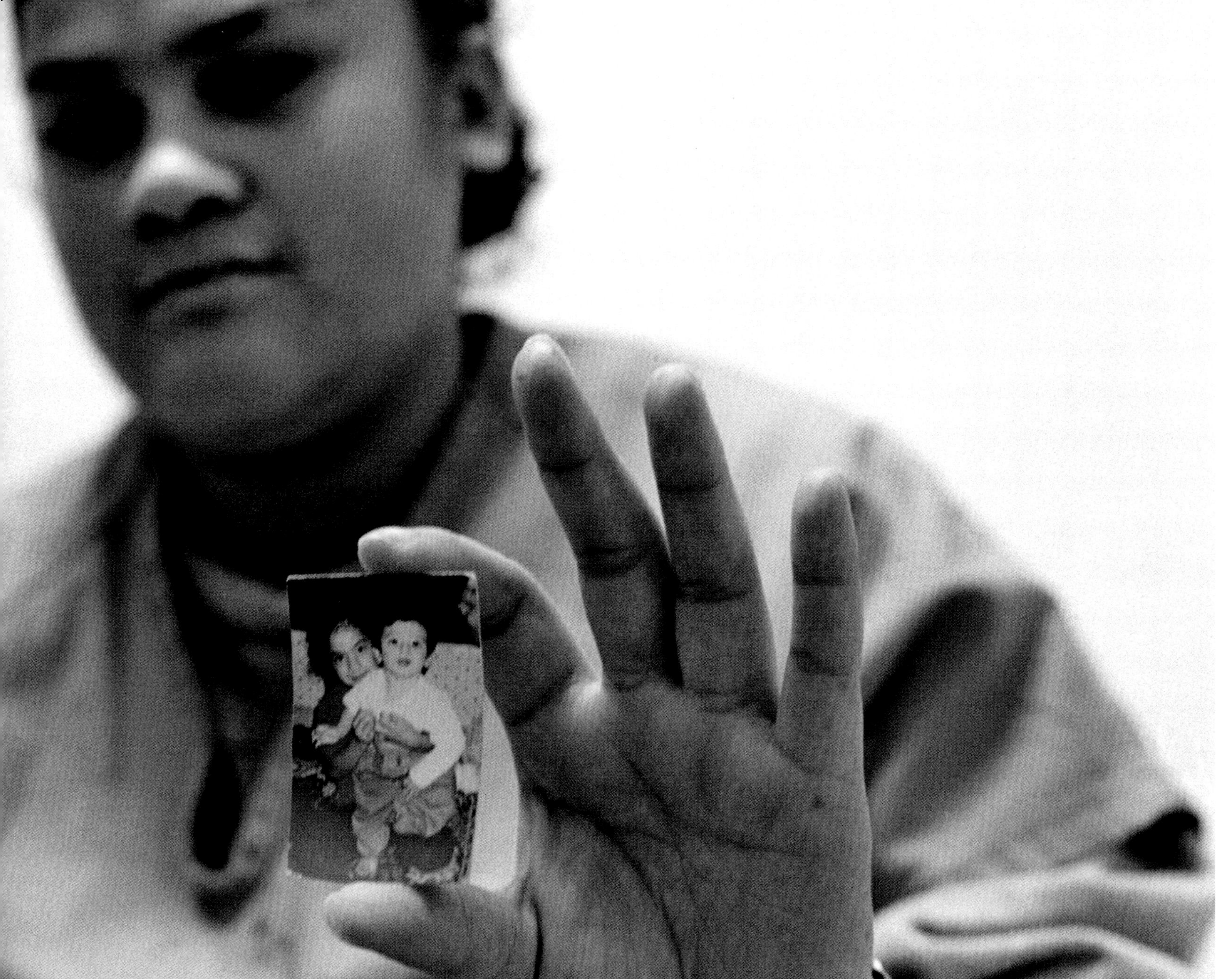

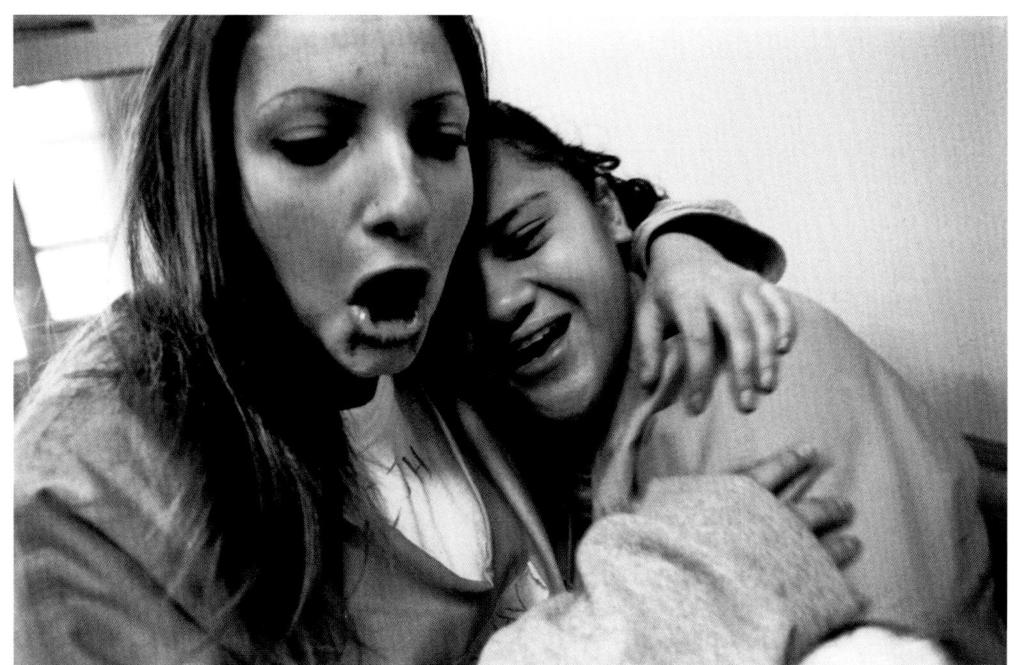
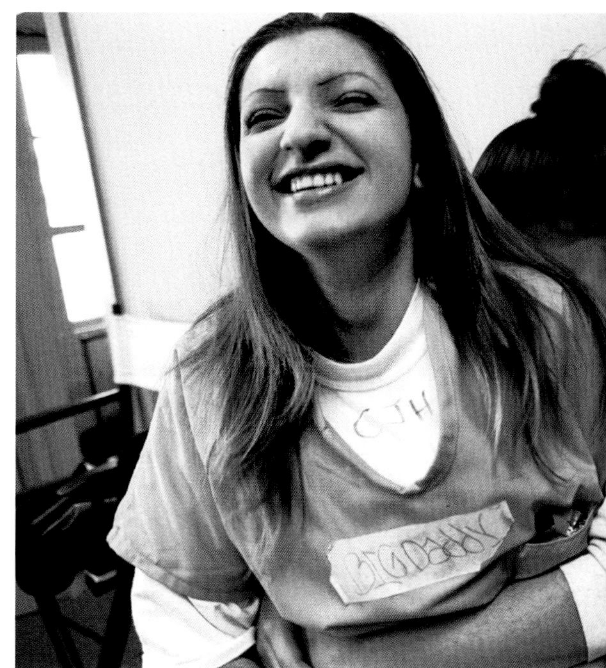

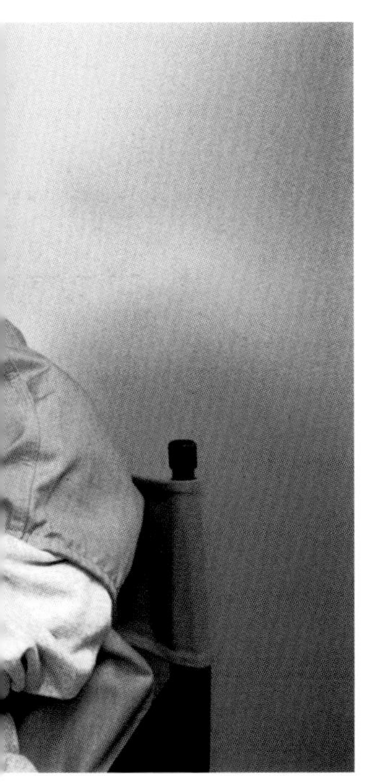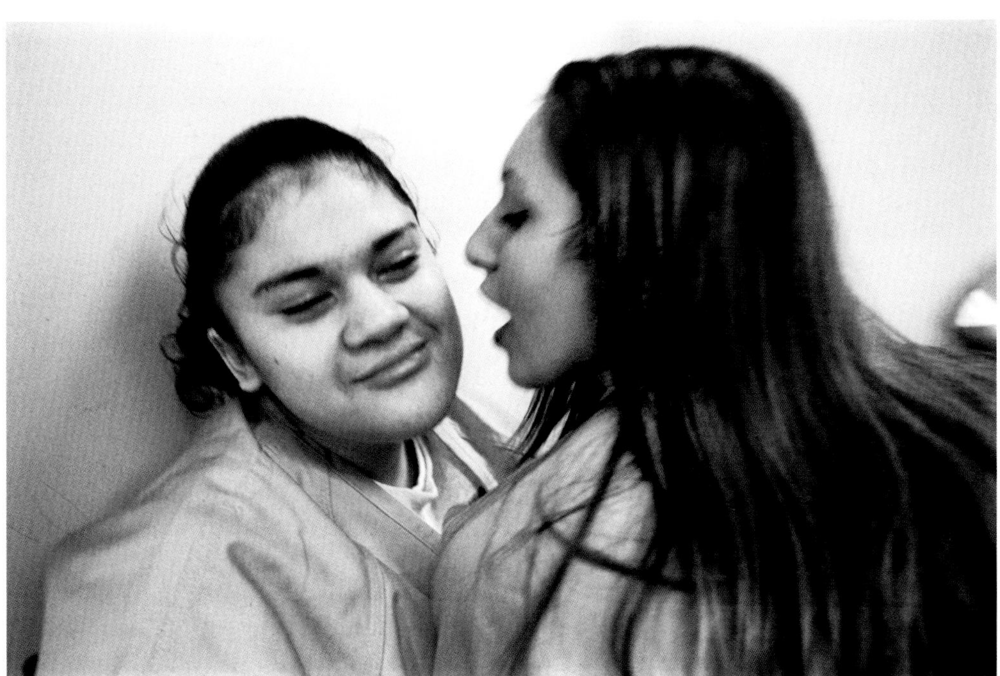

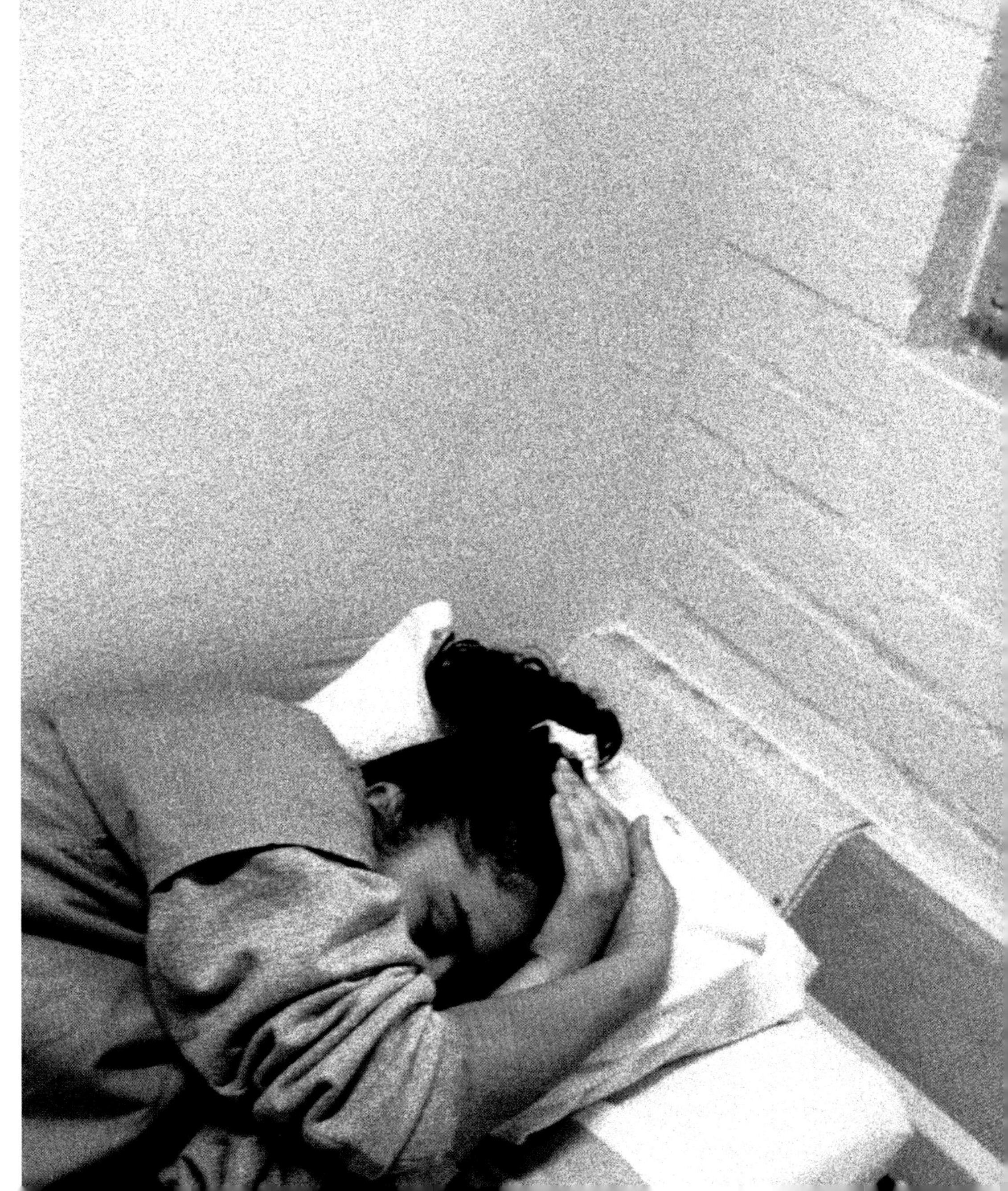

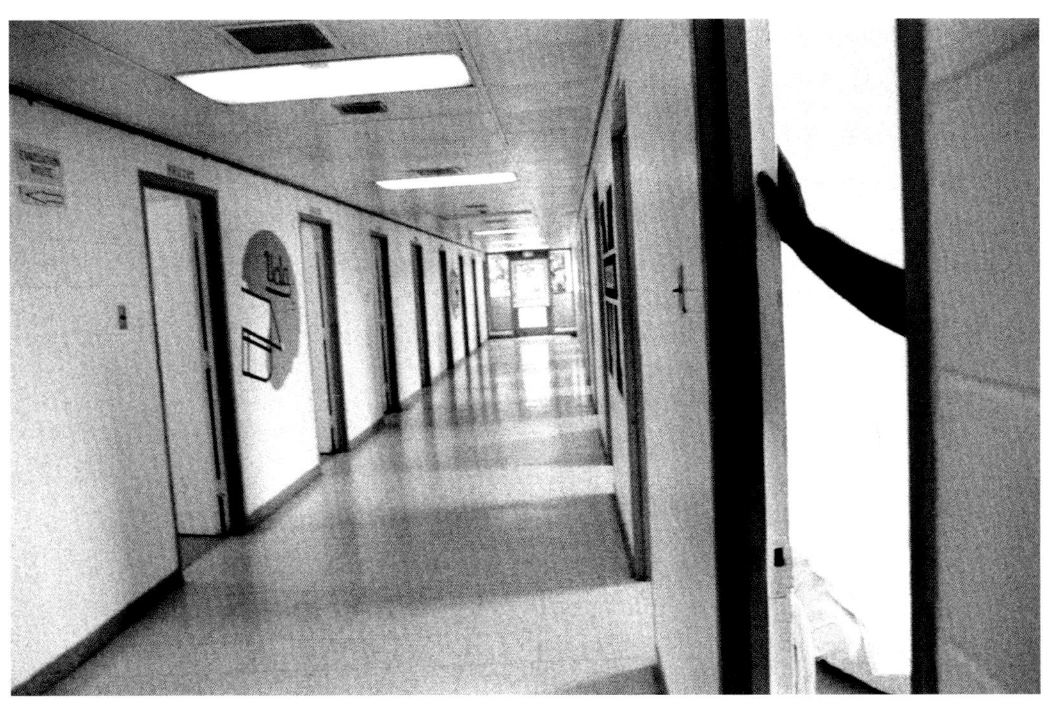

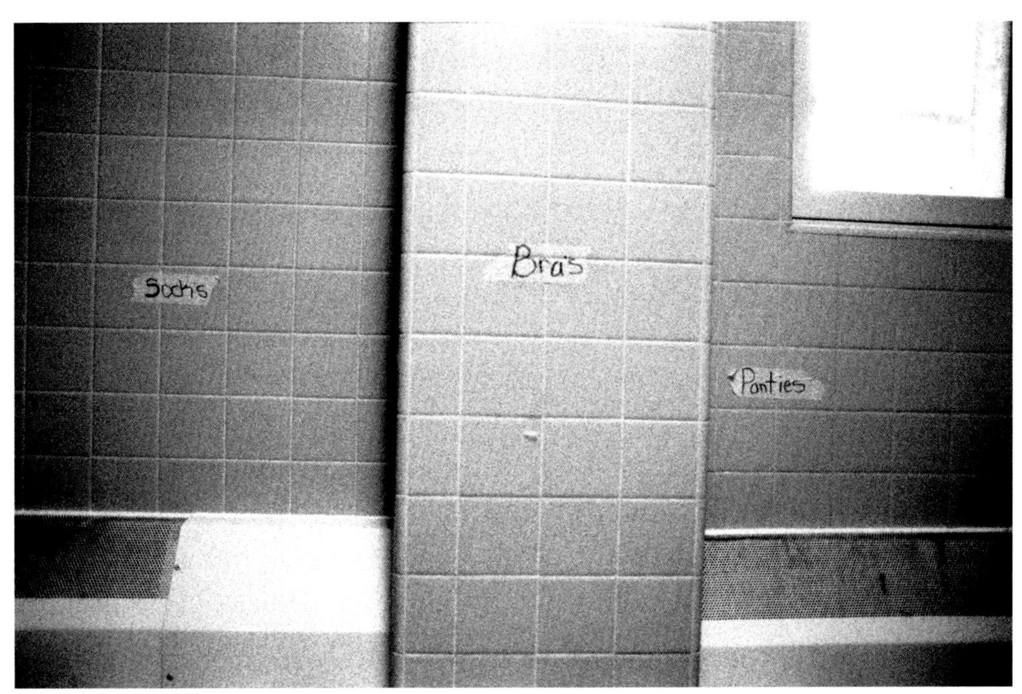

Socks
Bra's
Panties

Within three years of
their release, two out of
three former prisoners are
rearrested and 50% are
incarcerated again.

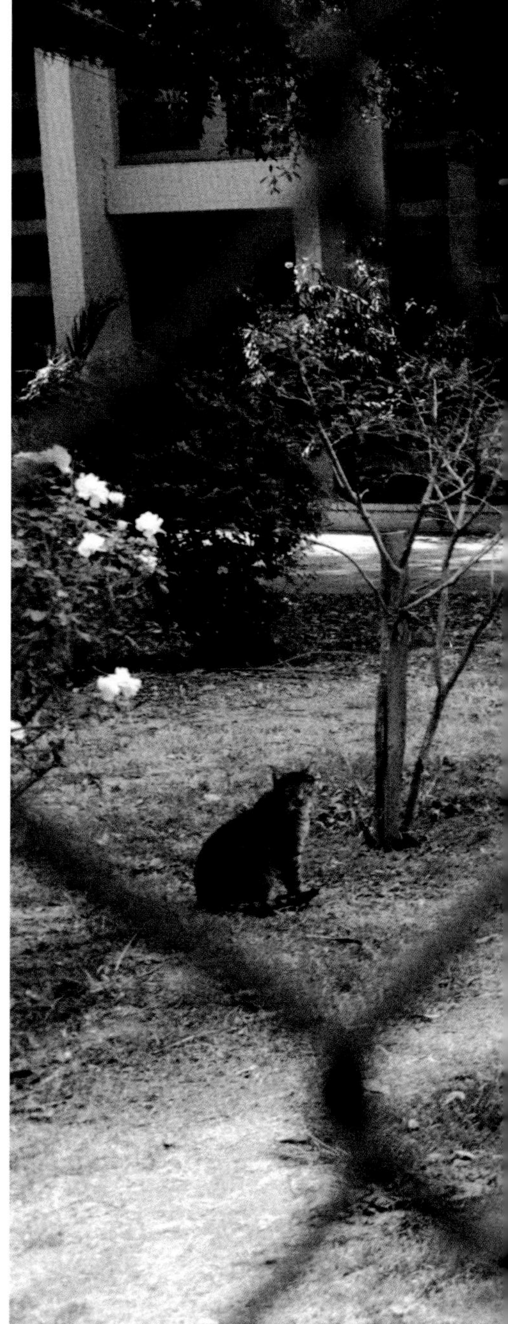

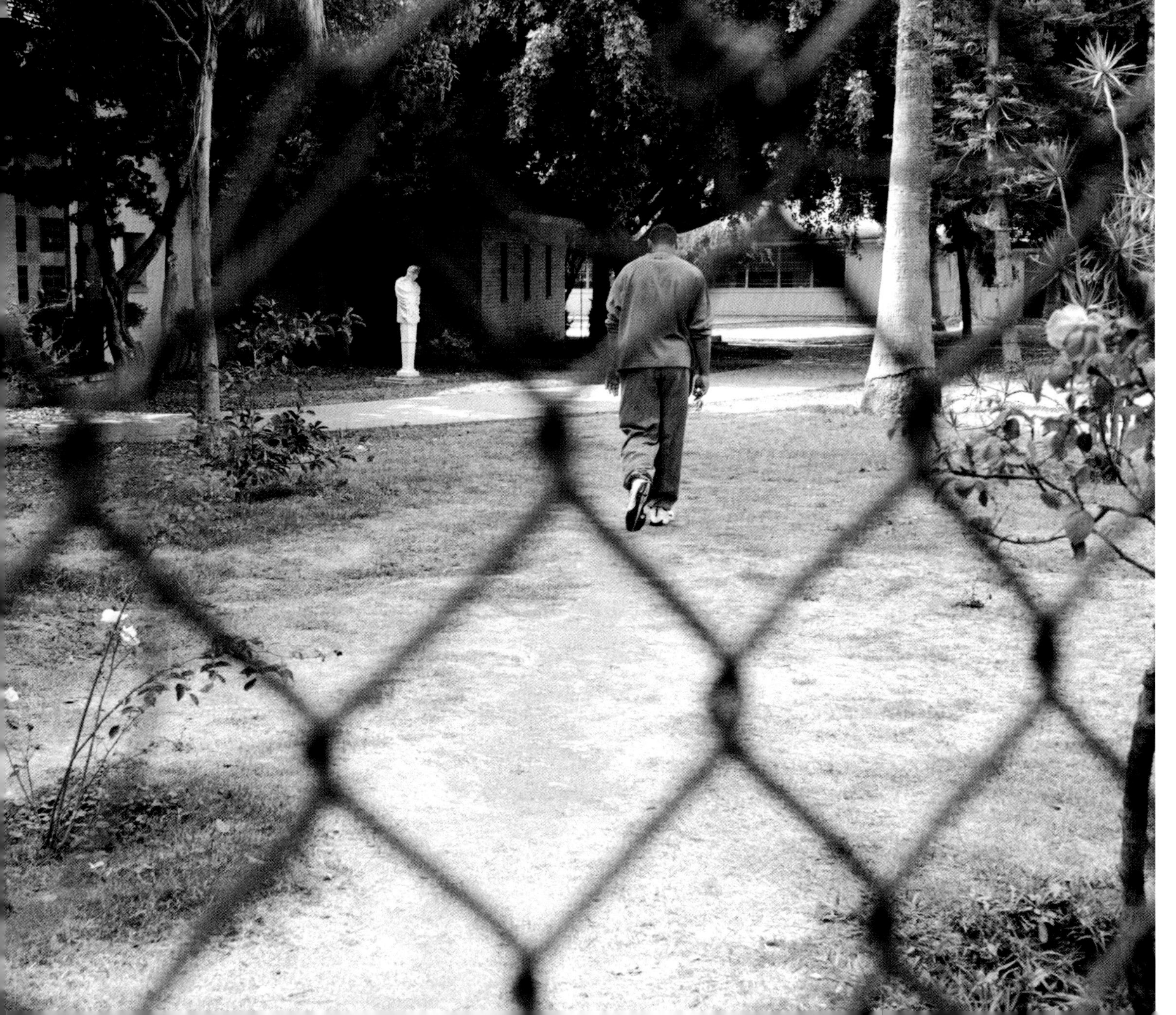

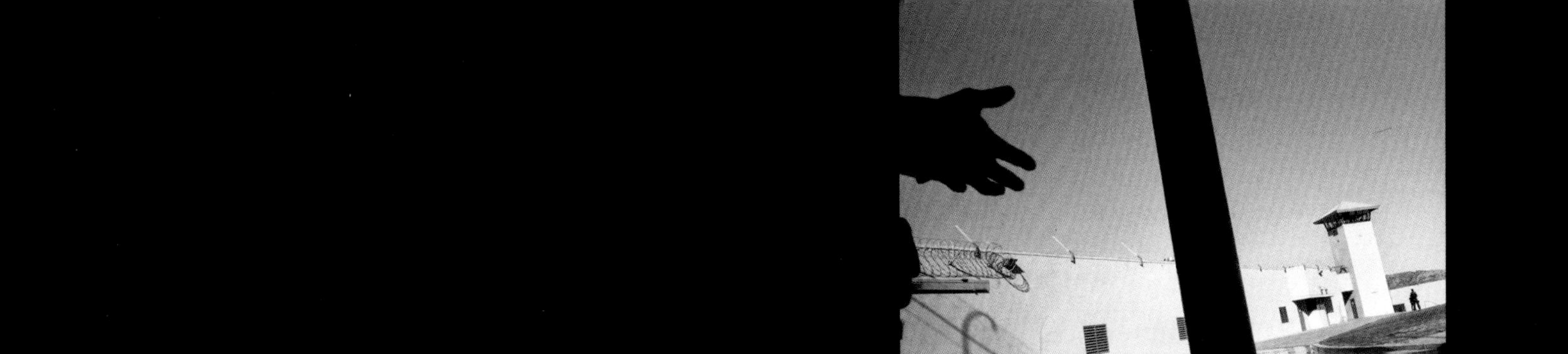

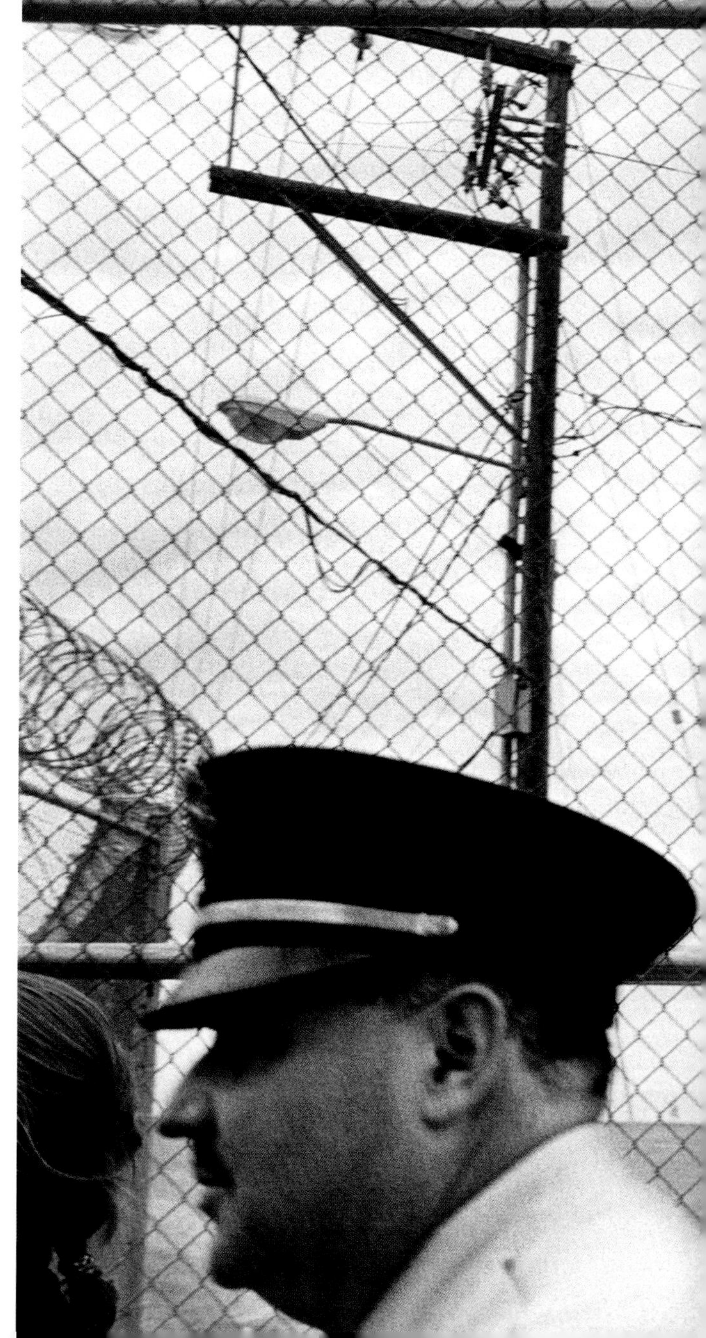

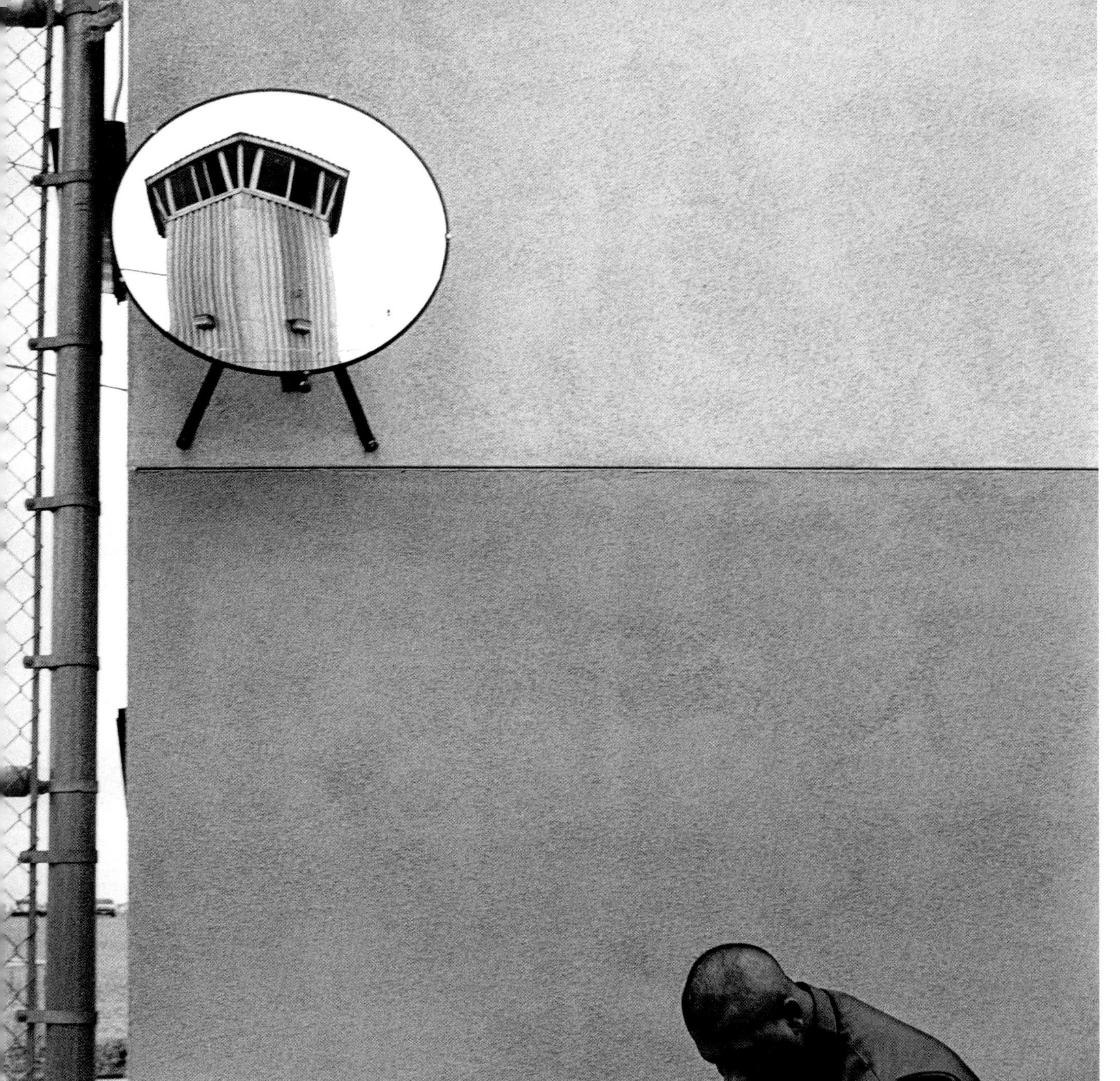

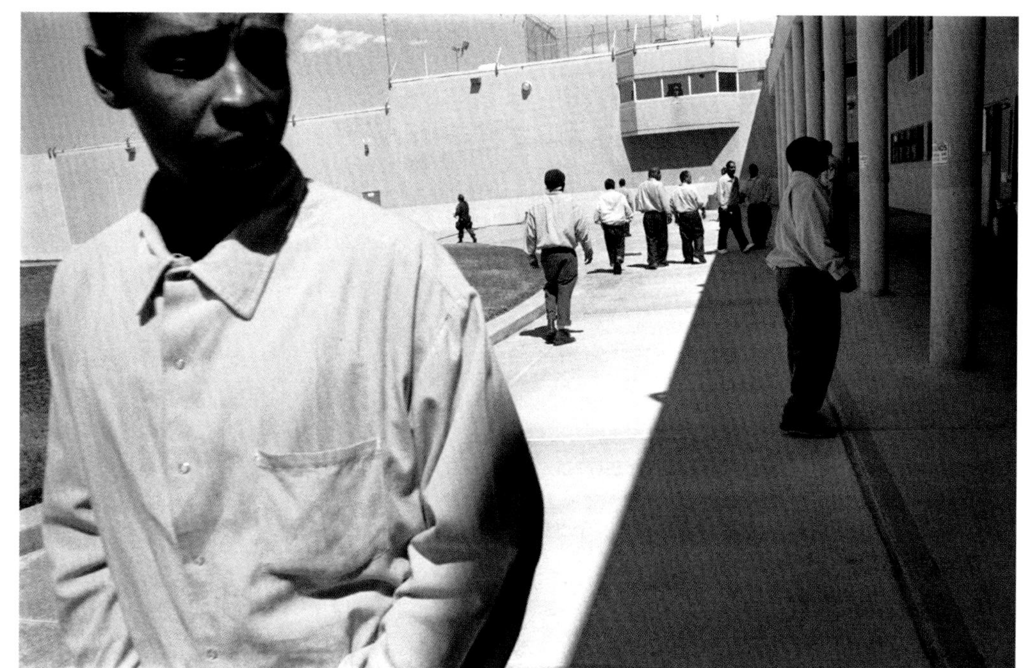
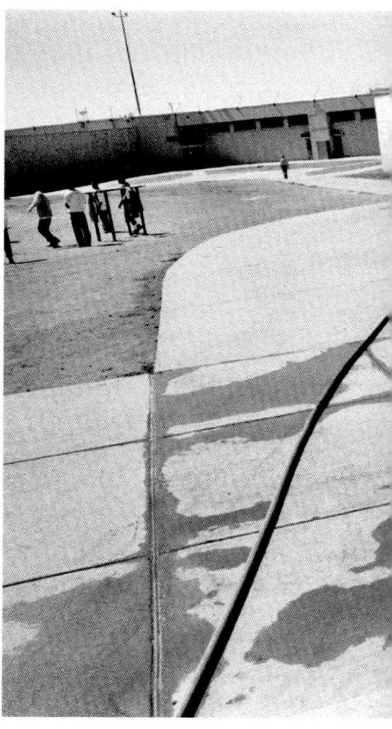

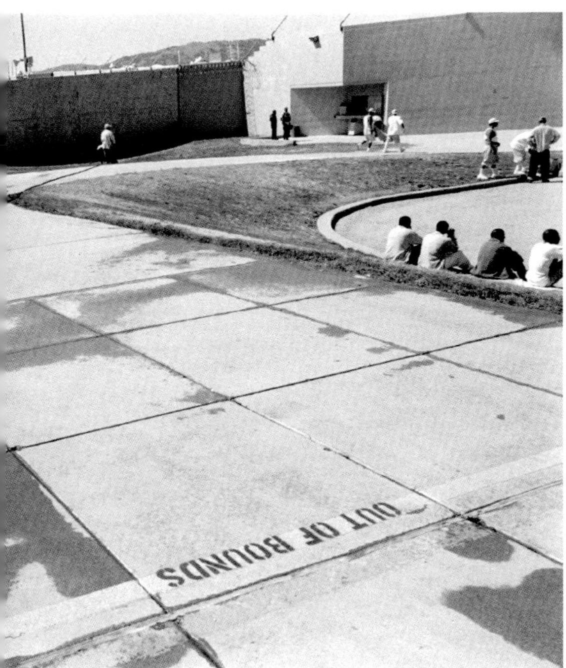
OUT OF BOUNDS

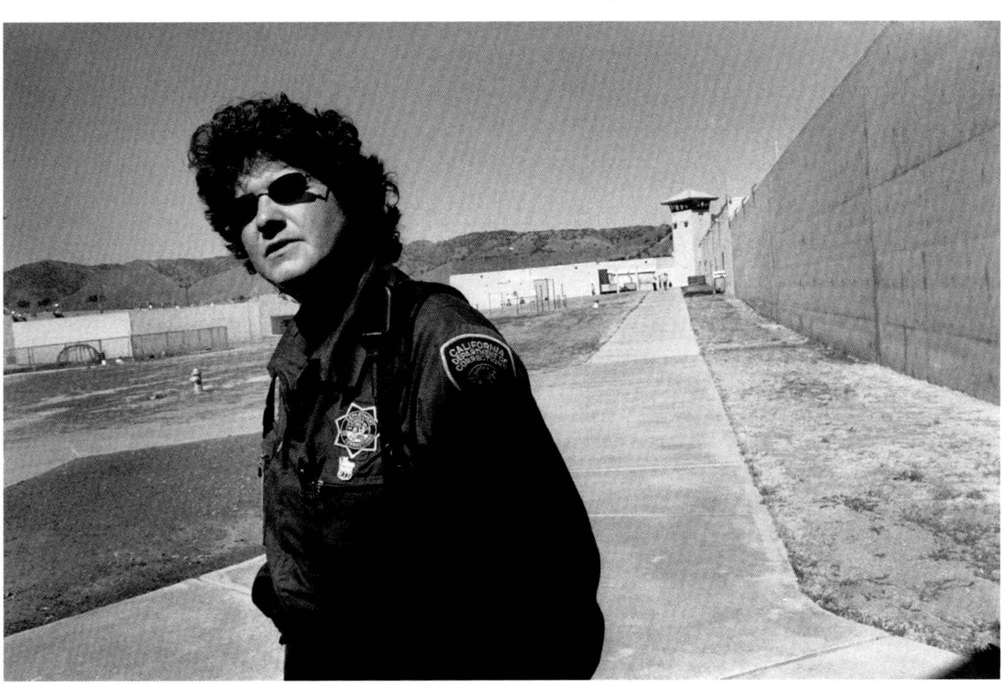
CALIFORNIA
DEPARTMENT OF
CORRECTIONS

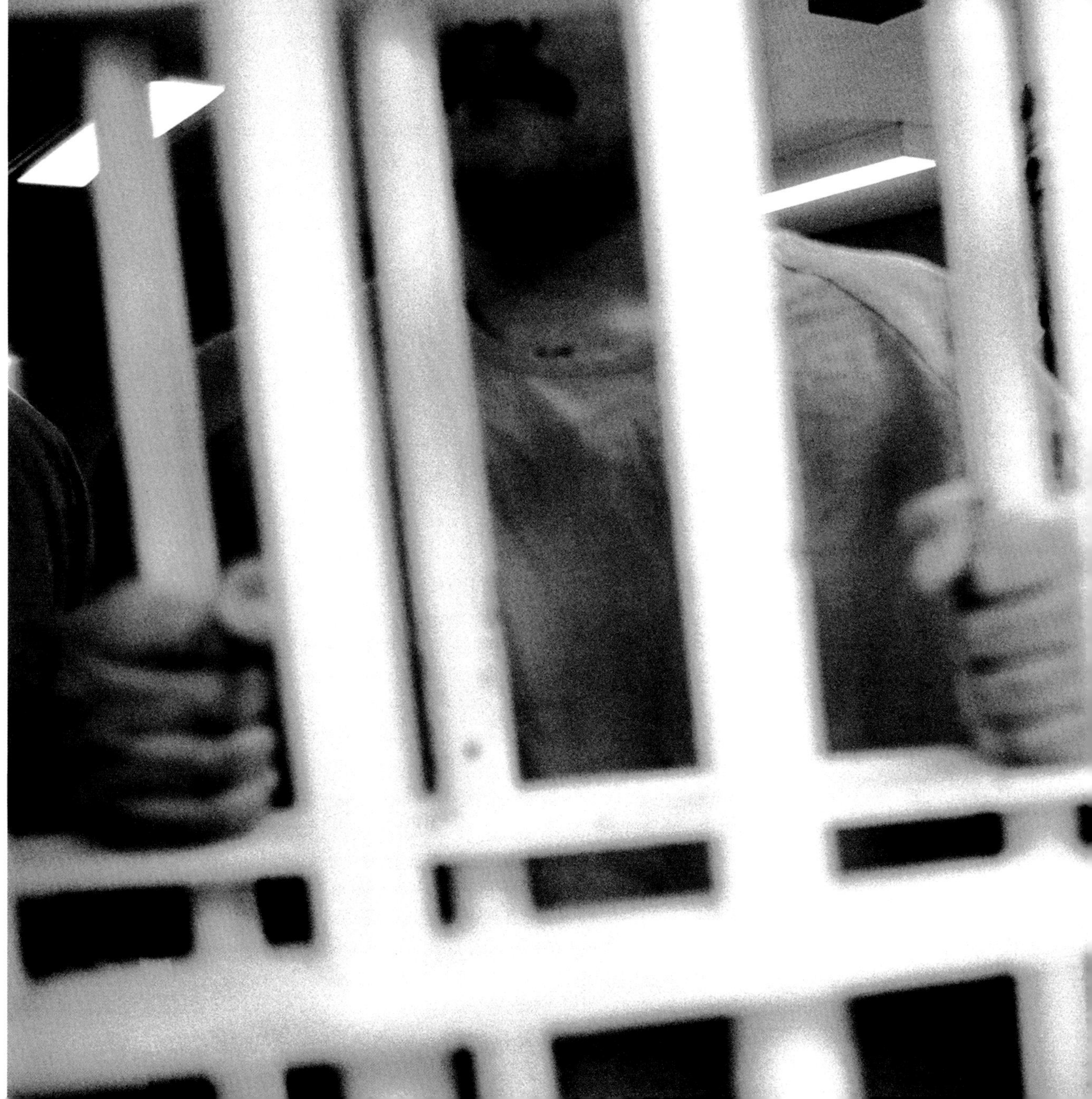

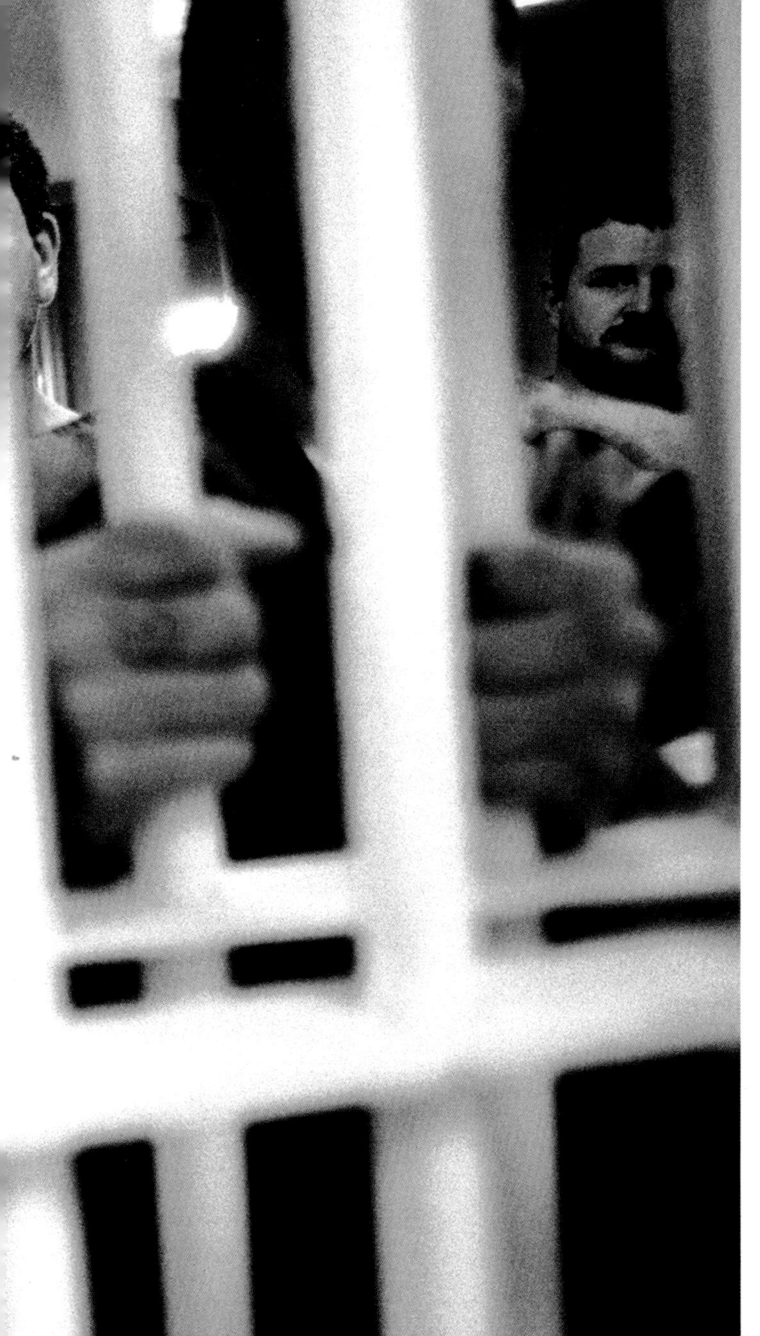

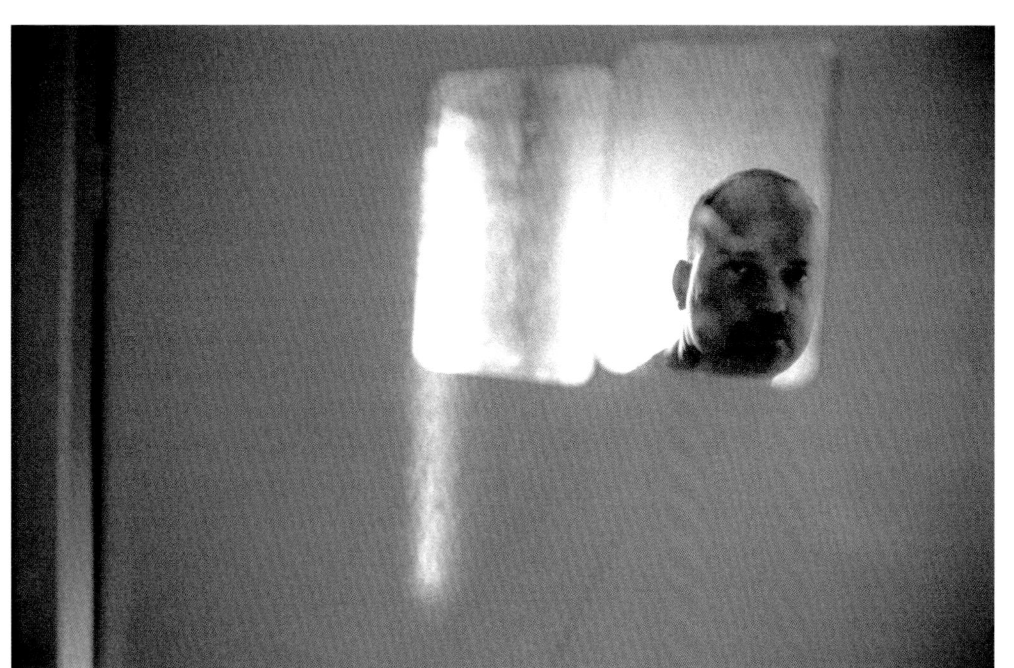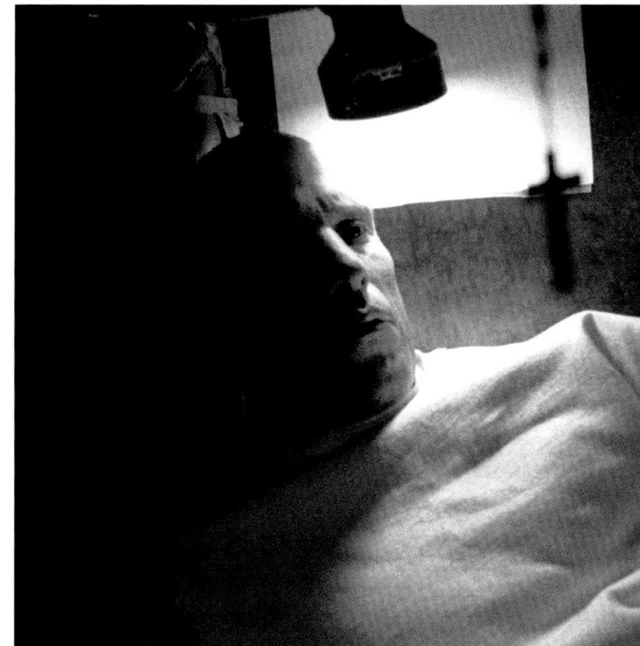

<u>FUCK!!</u>

FUCK THIS PIACE

FUCK EVERY ONE HEAR

FUCK, FUCK, FUCK

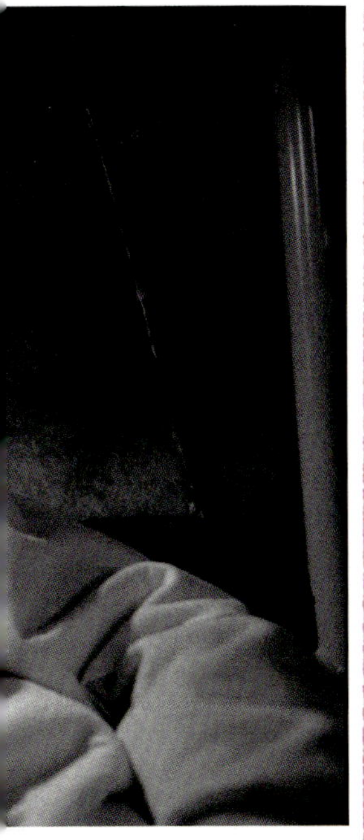

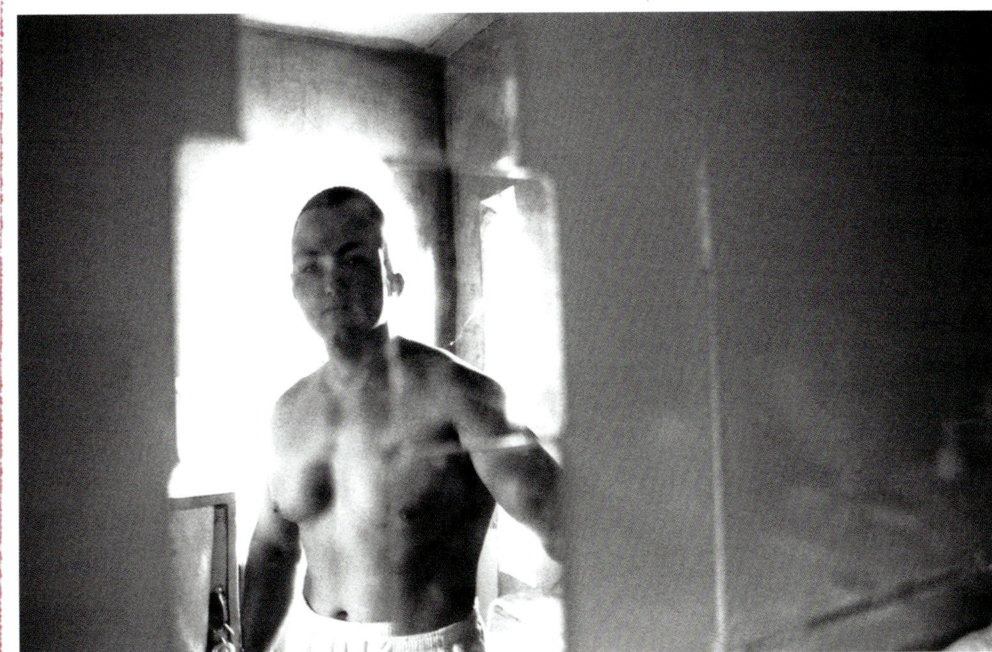

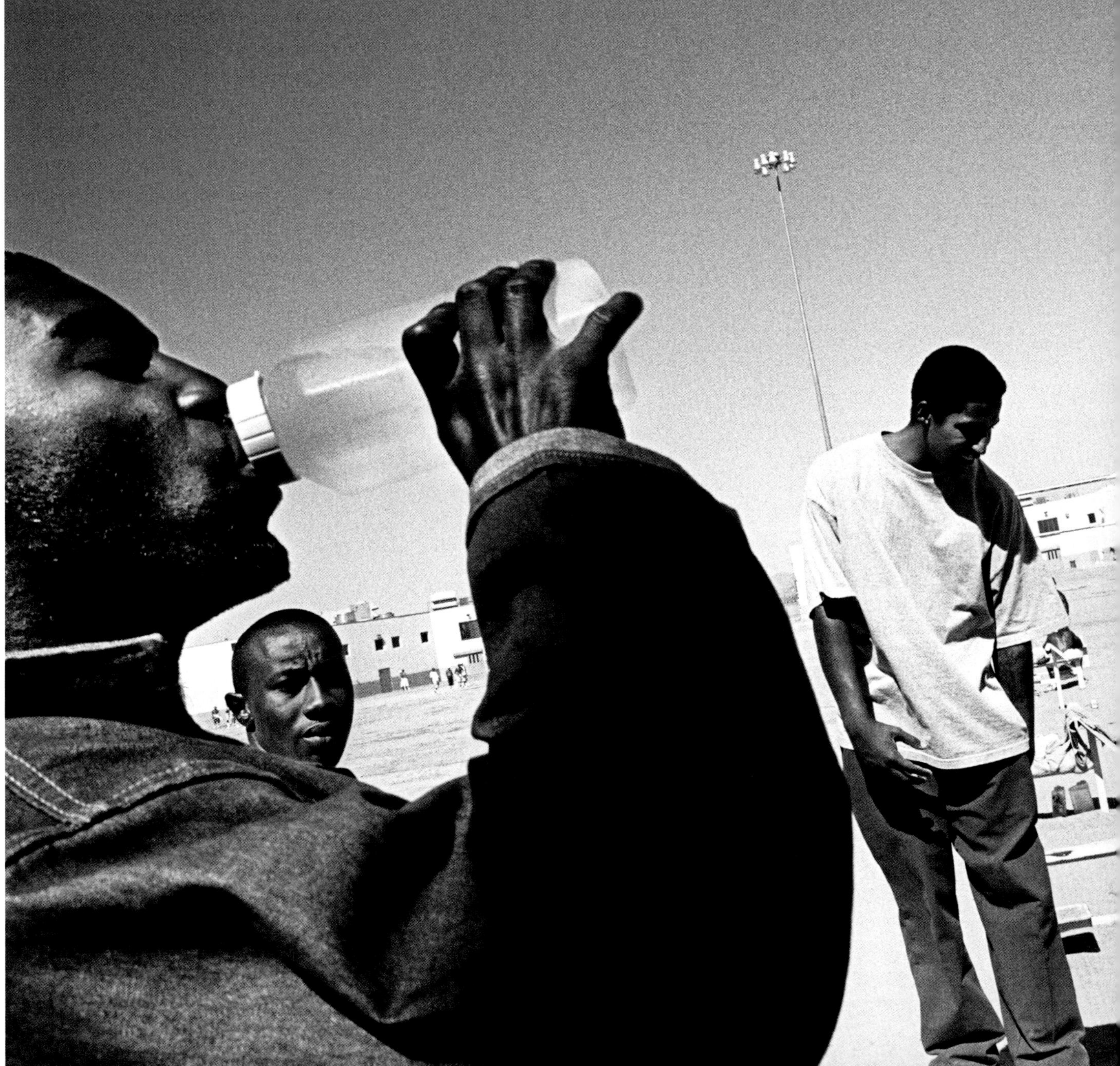

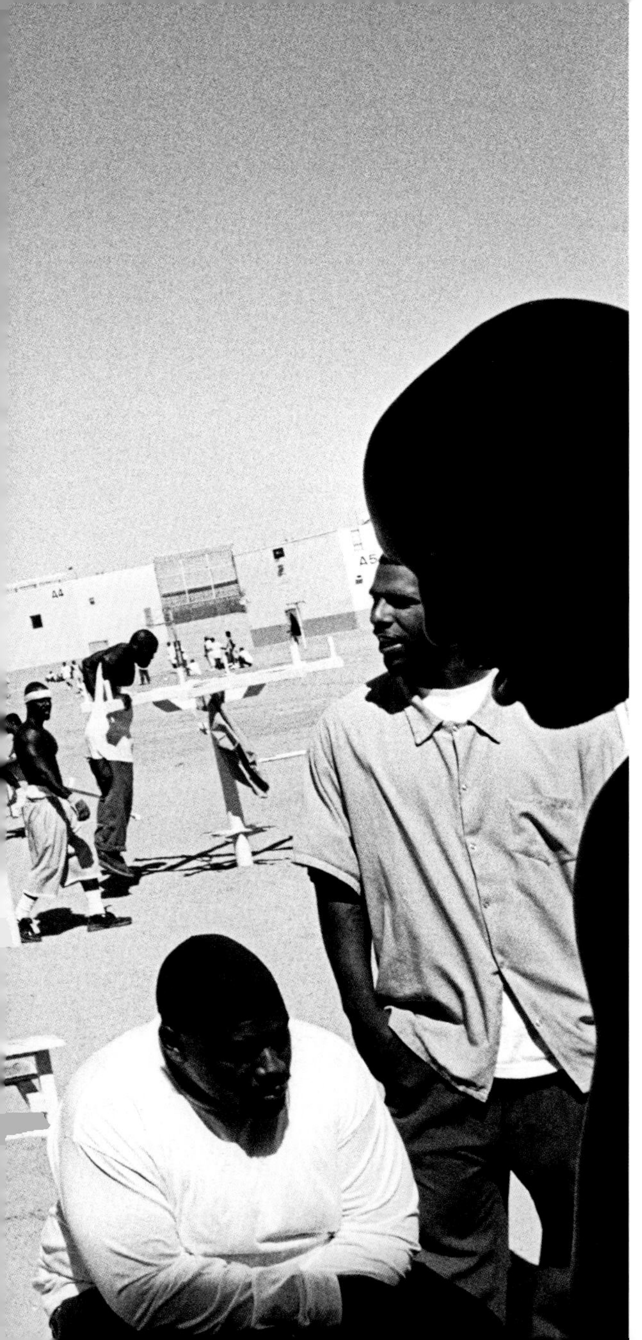

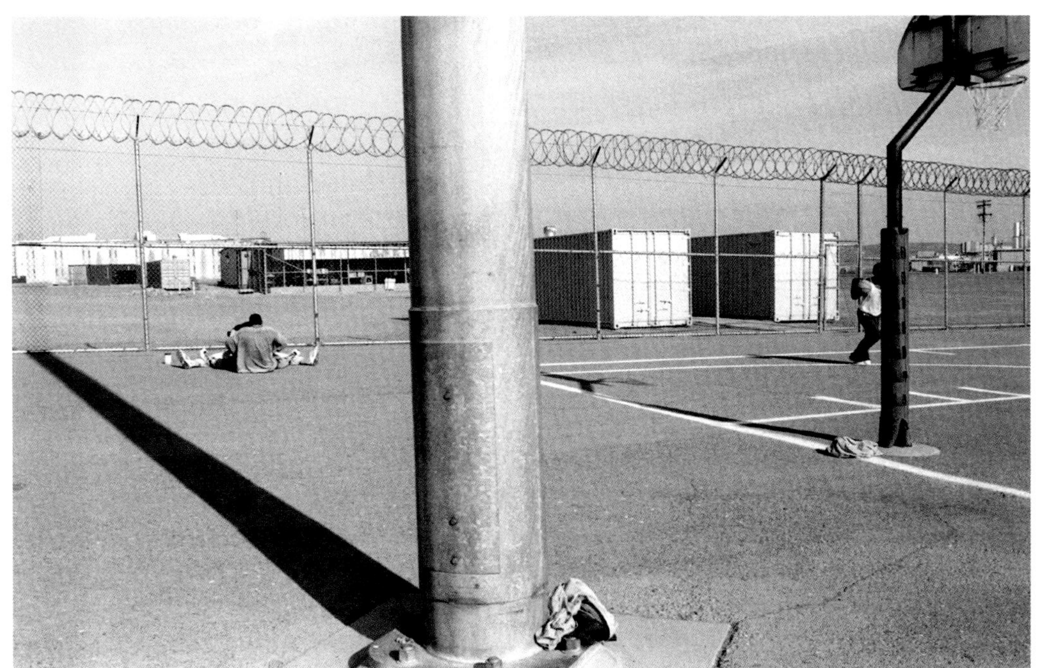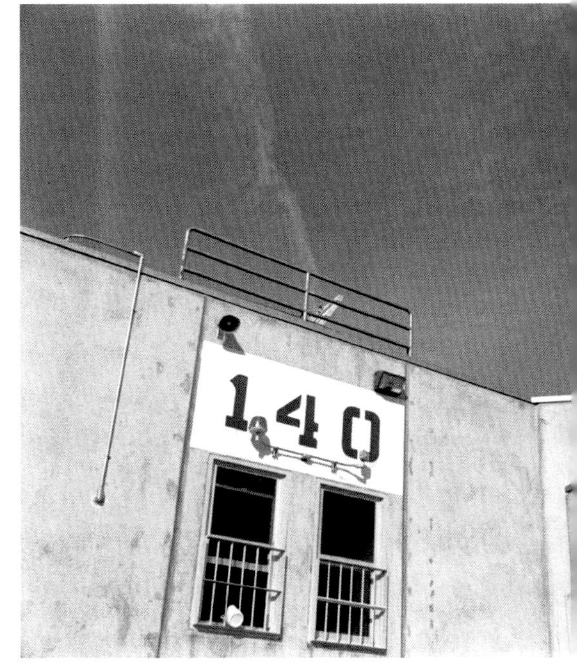

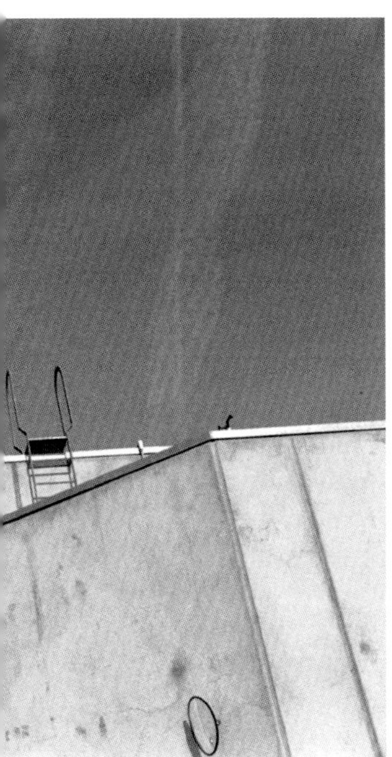
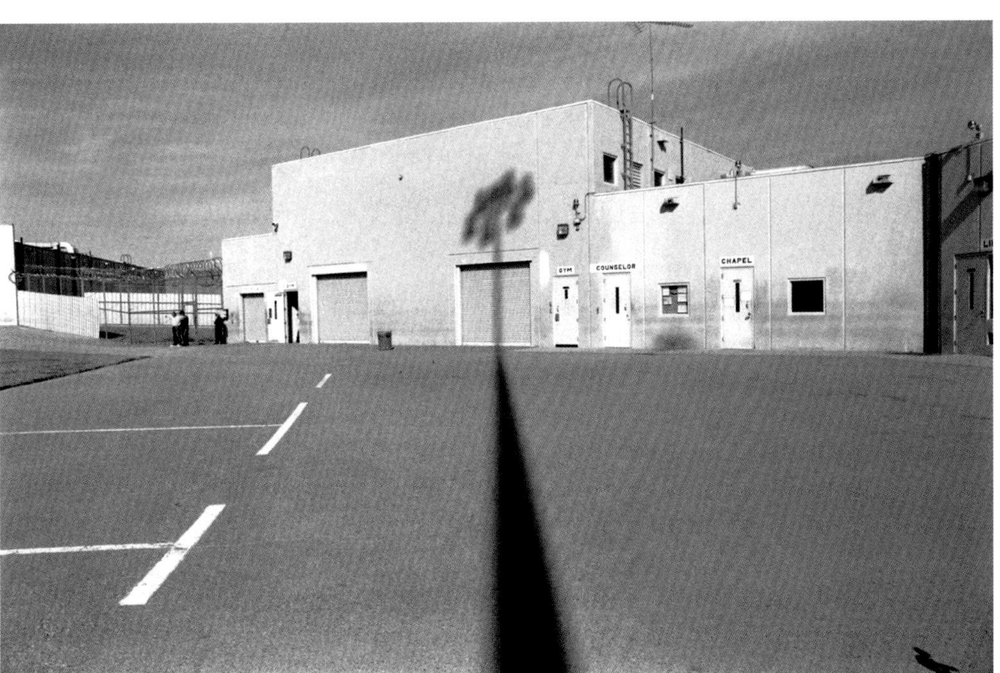

GYM
COUNSELOR
CHAPEL

It costs $336,000
a year to incarcerate
a youth in California.

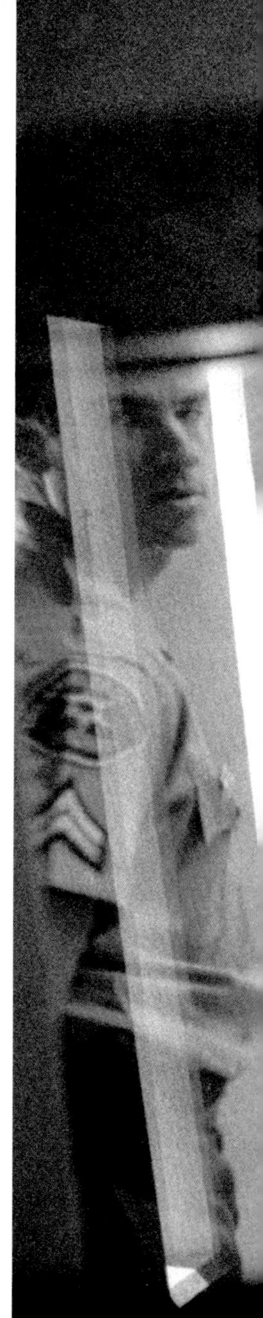

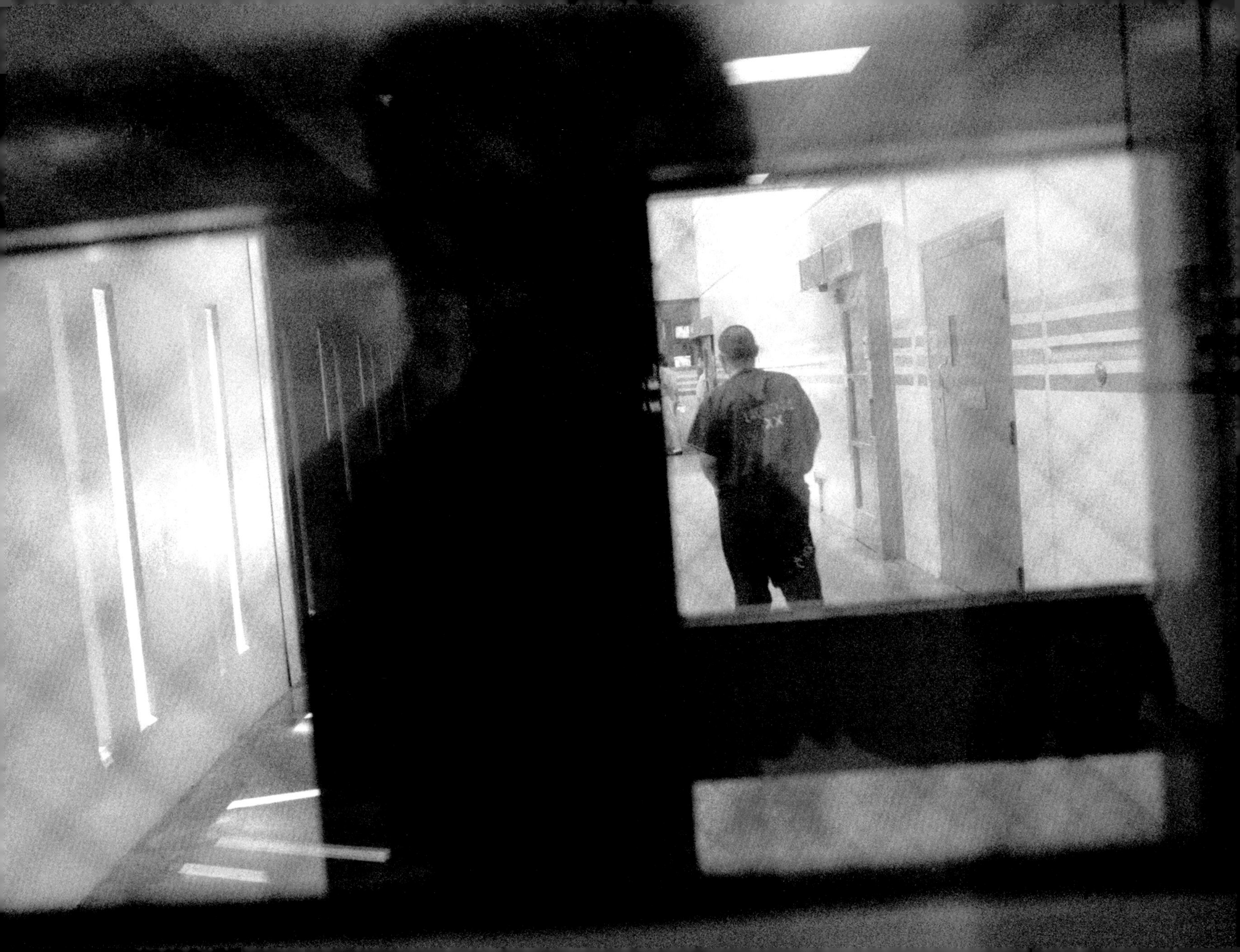

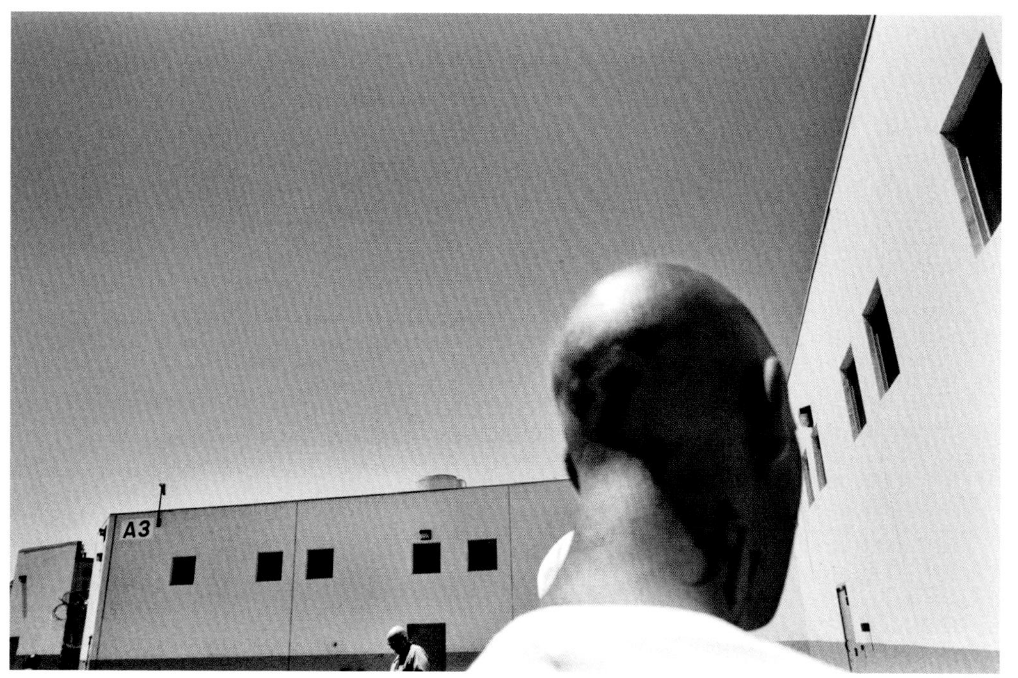
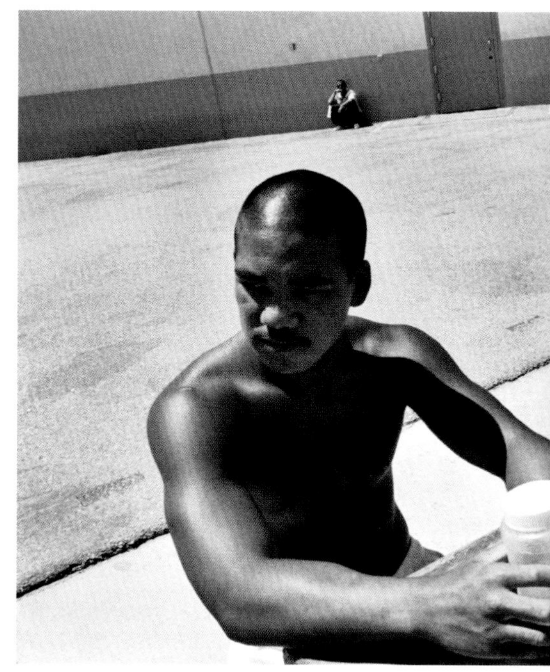

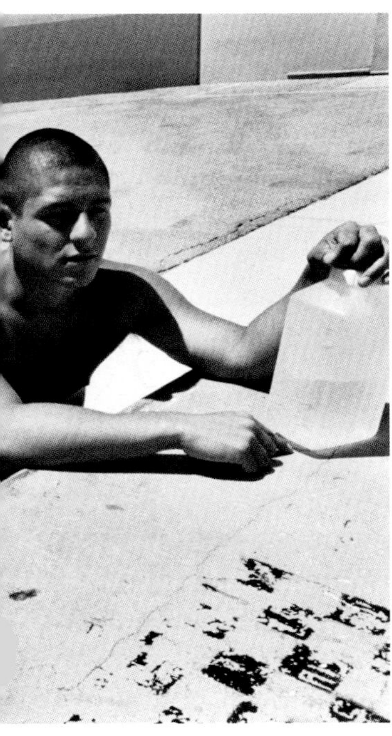
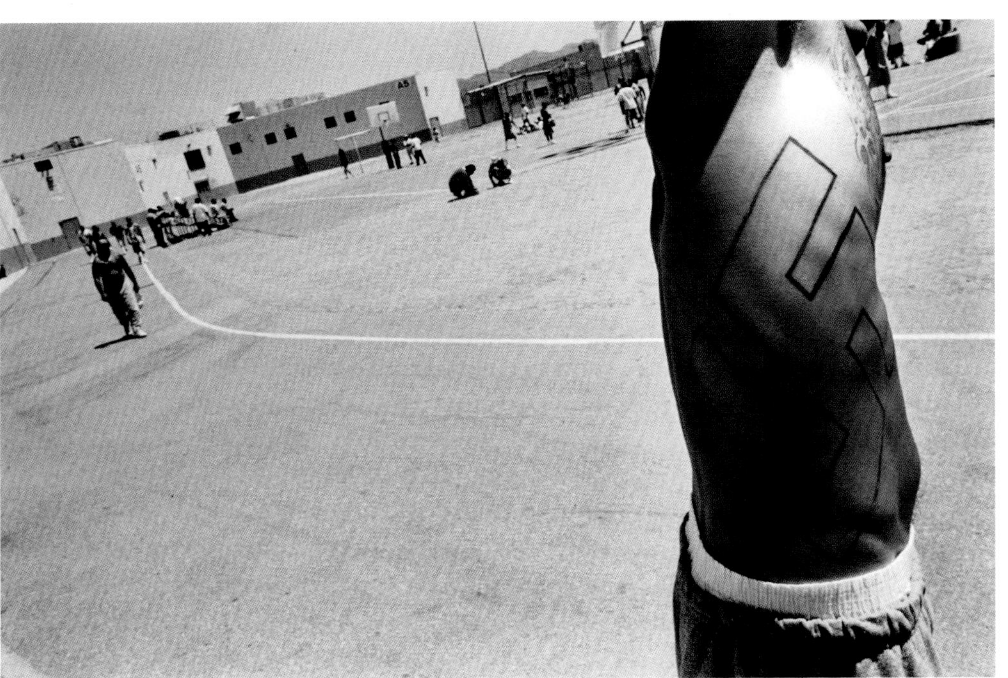

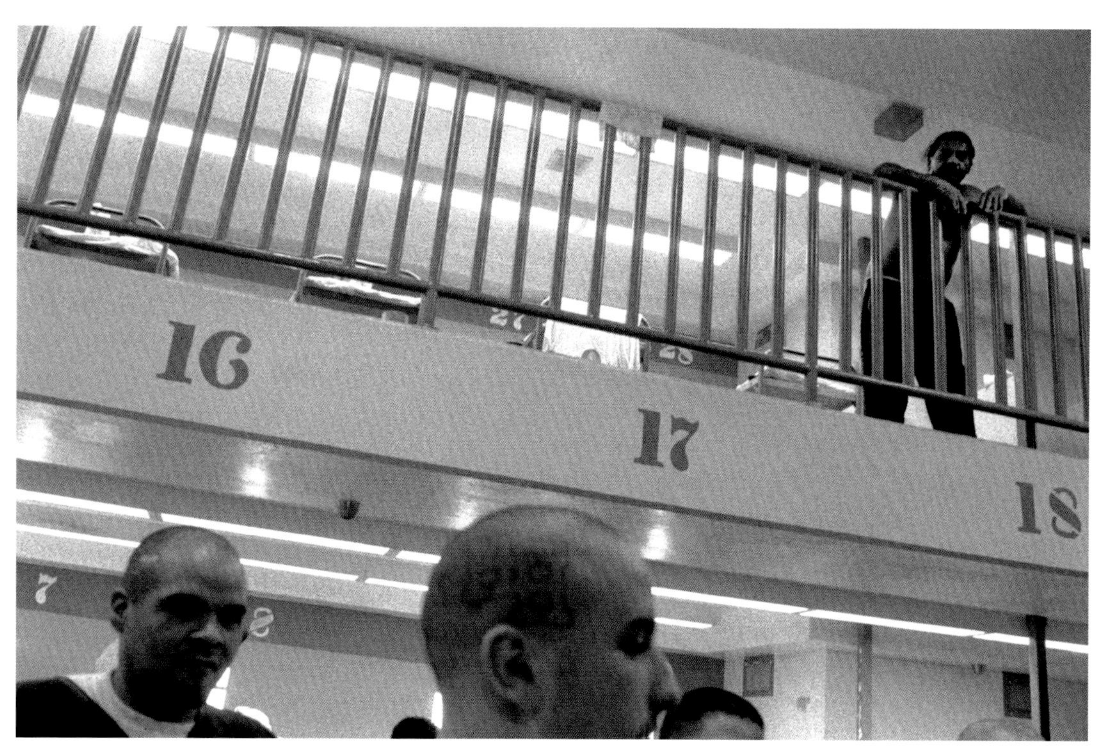
16
17
18
7

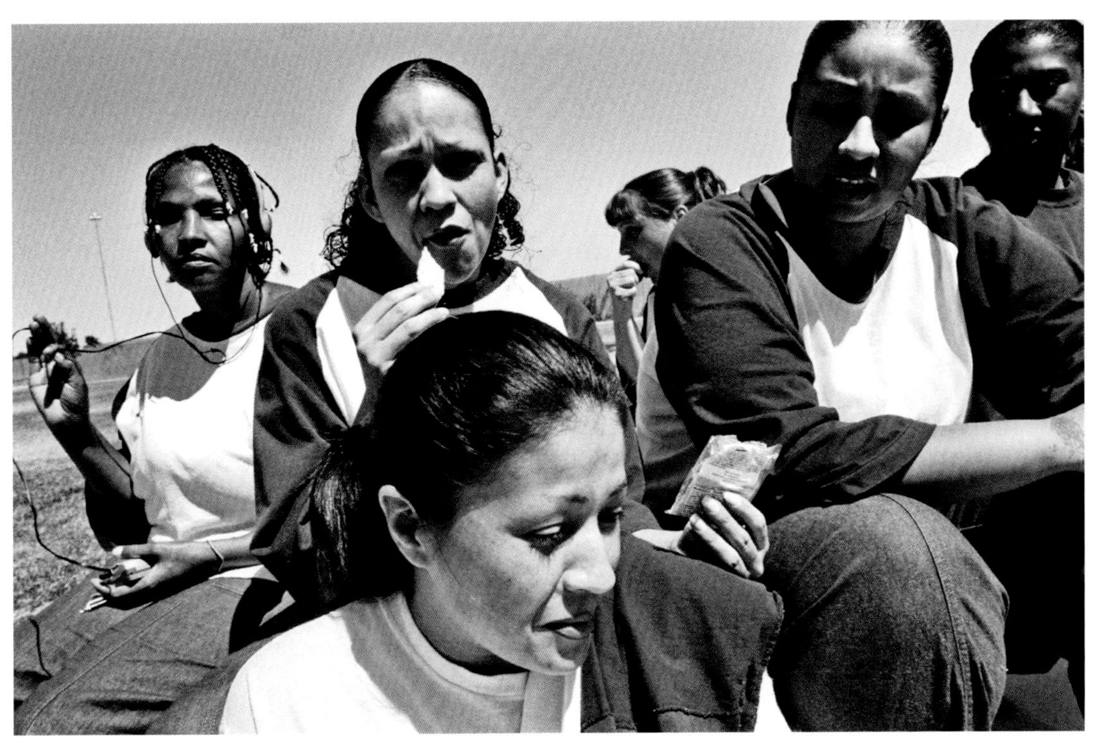

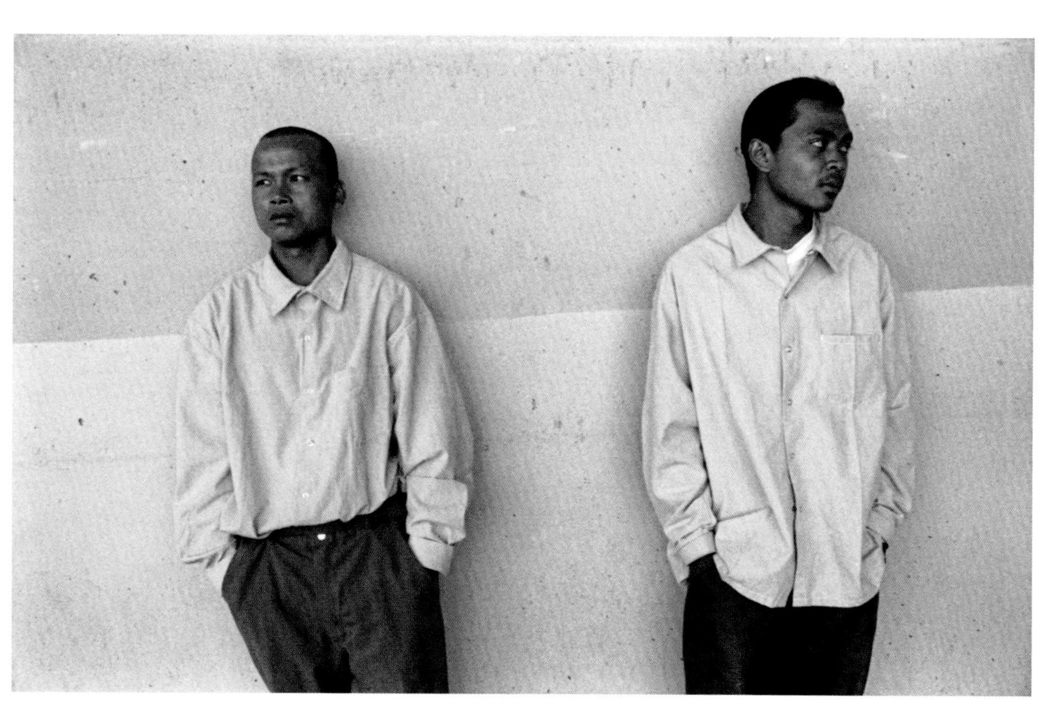

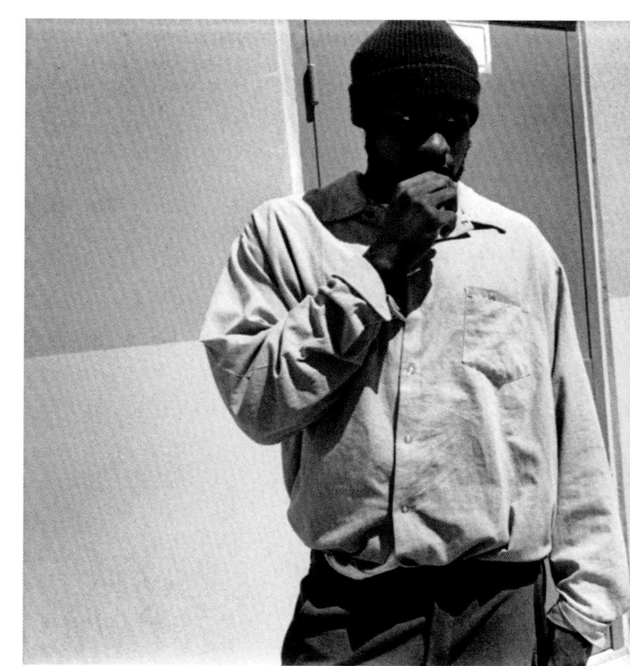

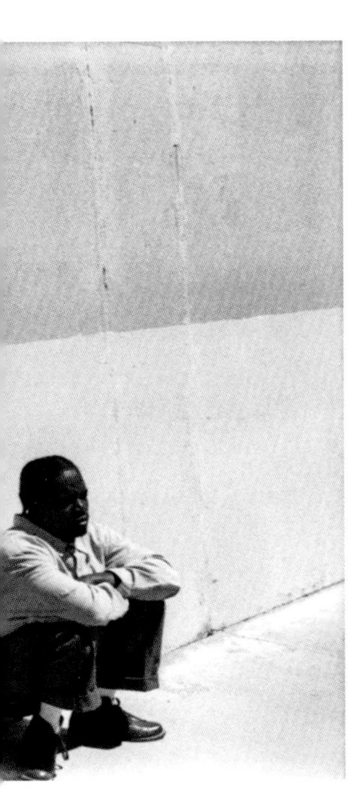
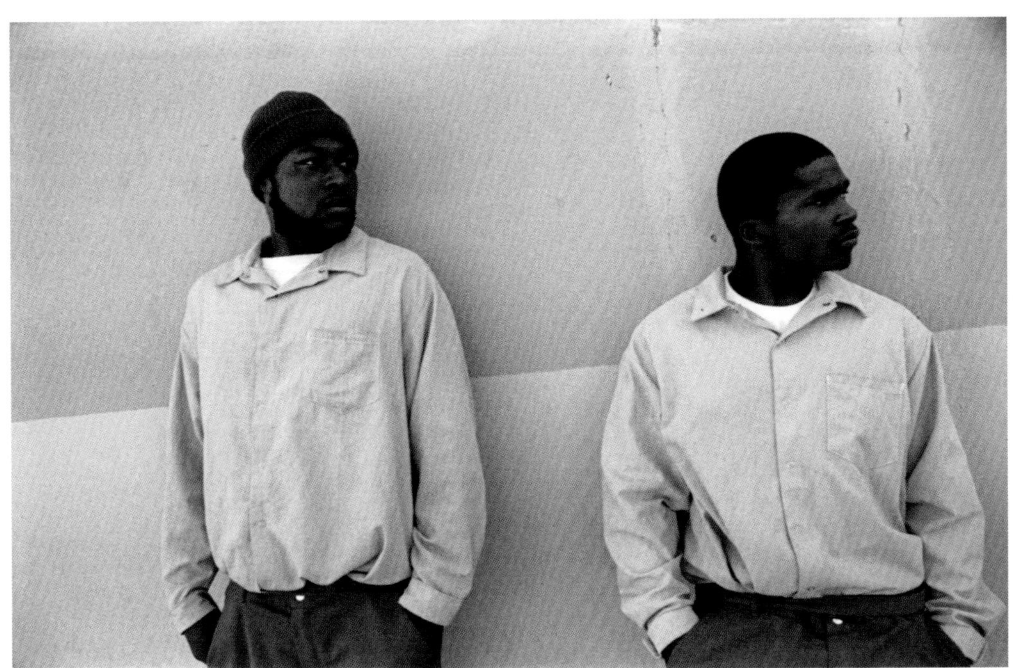

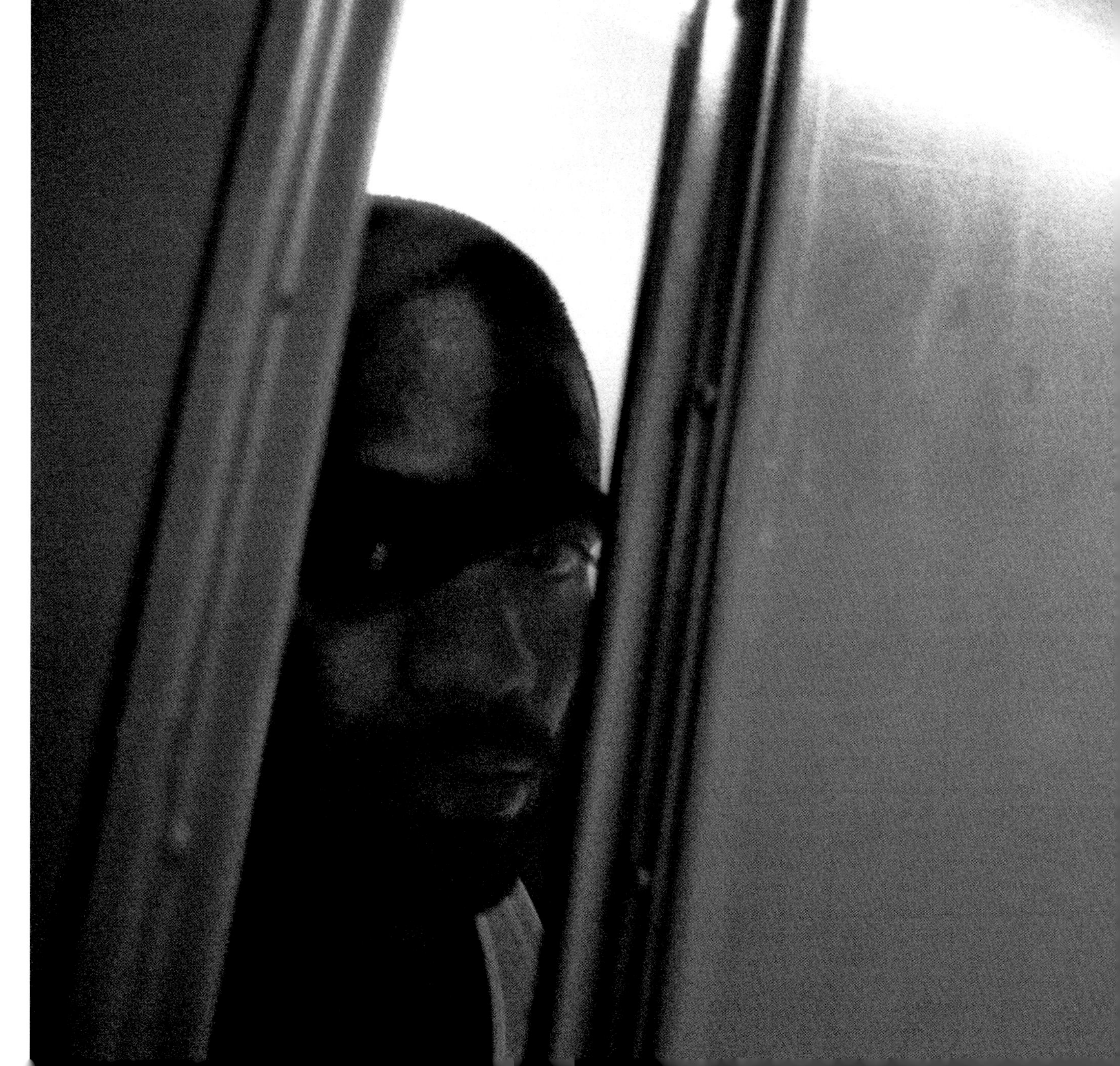

Youth in adult facilities
are thirty-six times more
likely to commit suicide and
are at the greatest risk of
sexual assault.

THERE IS
NO
WAY OUT
MY SCREAMS
HAVE
NO VOICE

I could be called a low life but life aint as low as me,
I am in juvenile hall headed for the penitentiary.

— George Trevino, sixteen years old: "Who Am I?"

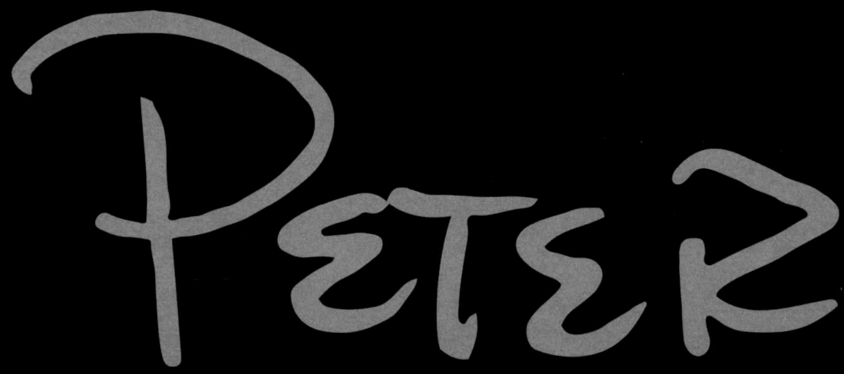

PETER
SEVENTEEN YEARS OLD

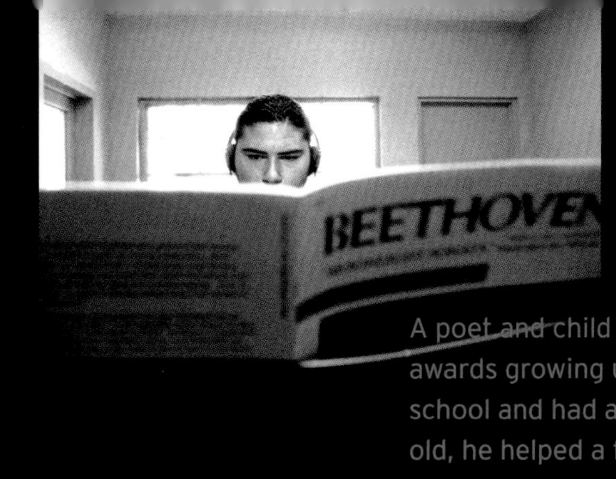

A poet and child musical prodigy, Peter won multiple awards growing up. He attended a private elementary school and had a supportive family. At sixteen years old, he helped a friend break into a house. When the owner unexpectedly came home, Peter struck him with a golf club and fled. Charged with breaking and entering and assault with a deadly weapon, Peter was facing thirty-five years to life. He took a twelve-year deal in adult prison. It was his first offense.

<A New Life>

My life, a tangled, disorganized, web of distrust and lies. No shame, no guilt, just my own welfare. I've looked deep into my fathers eyes, bypassing truth, not knowing that he knew the falseness of my words. My crooked days of sin have finally caught up with me — let them take their toll, for nothing, not even Satan Himself can break my will to live ~~because the sin~~ of righteousness; because the evil get what they fear, and what scares me the most is my father's death.

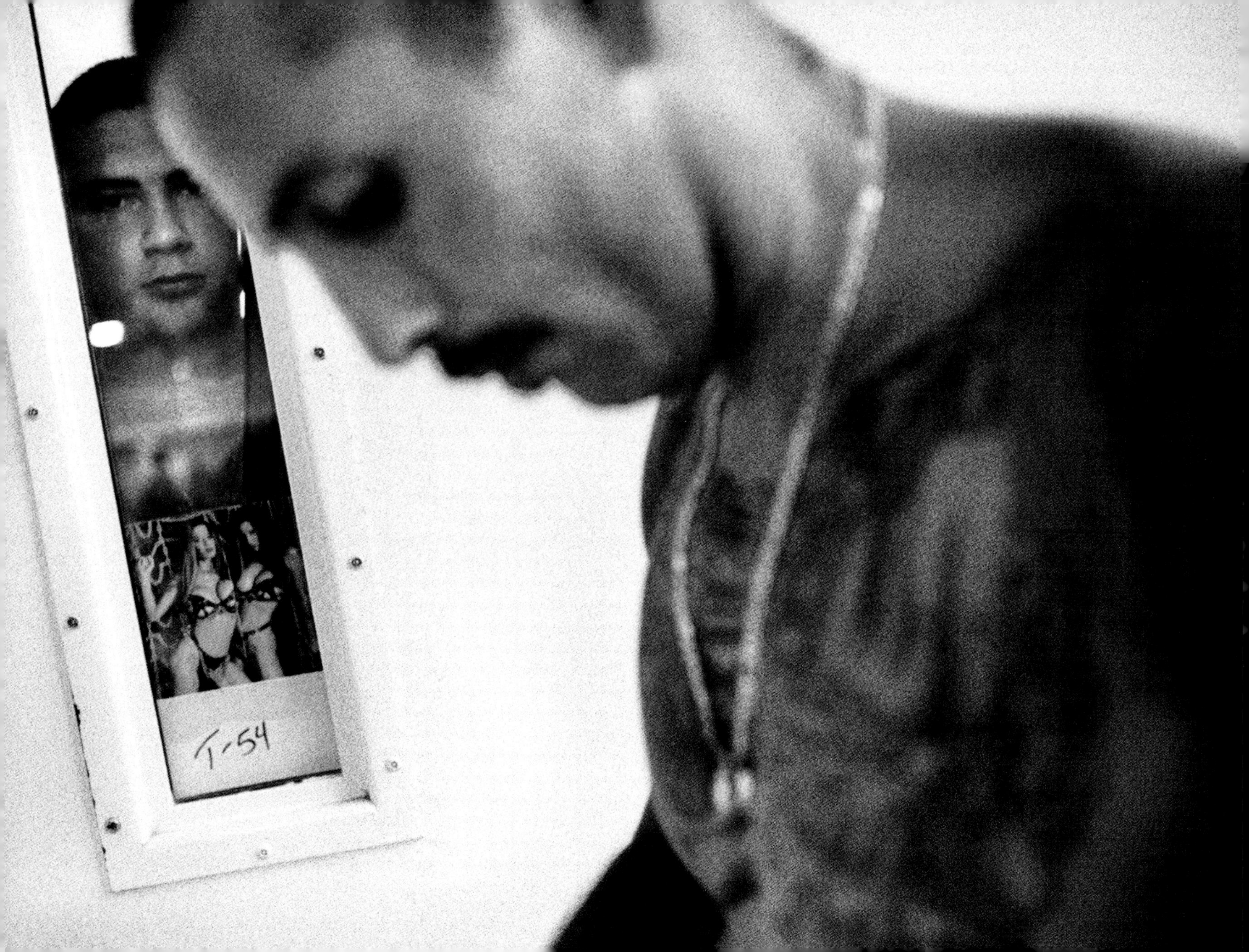
T-54

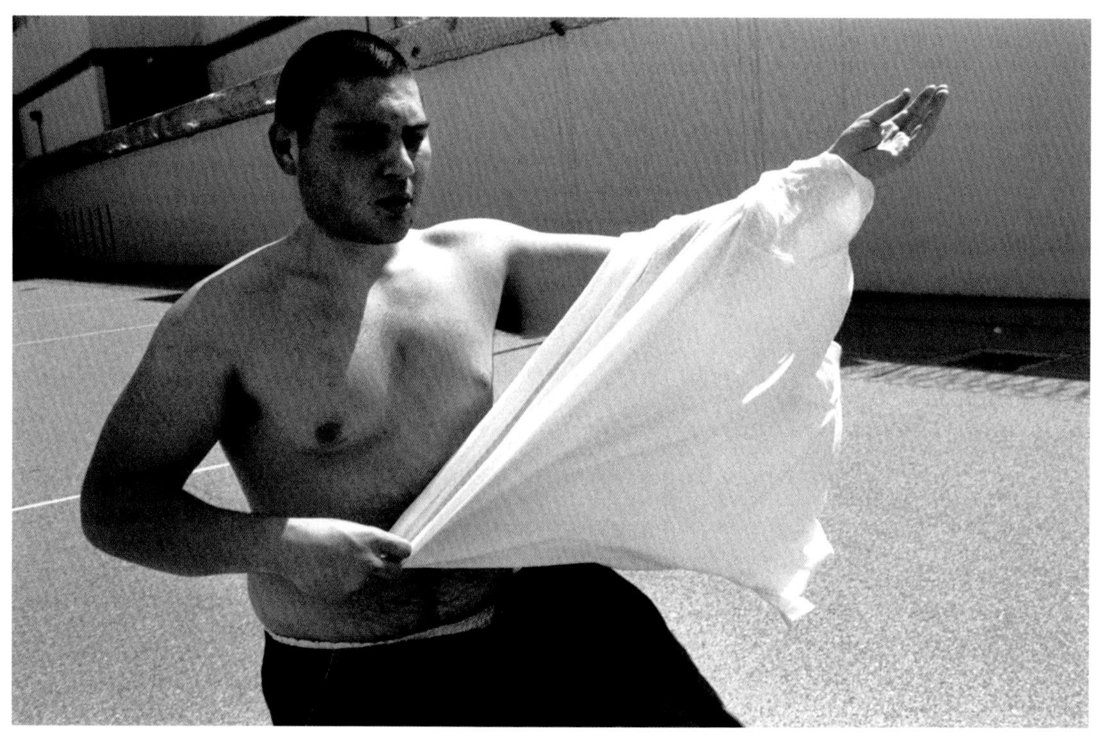

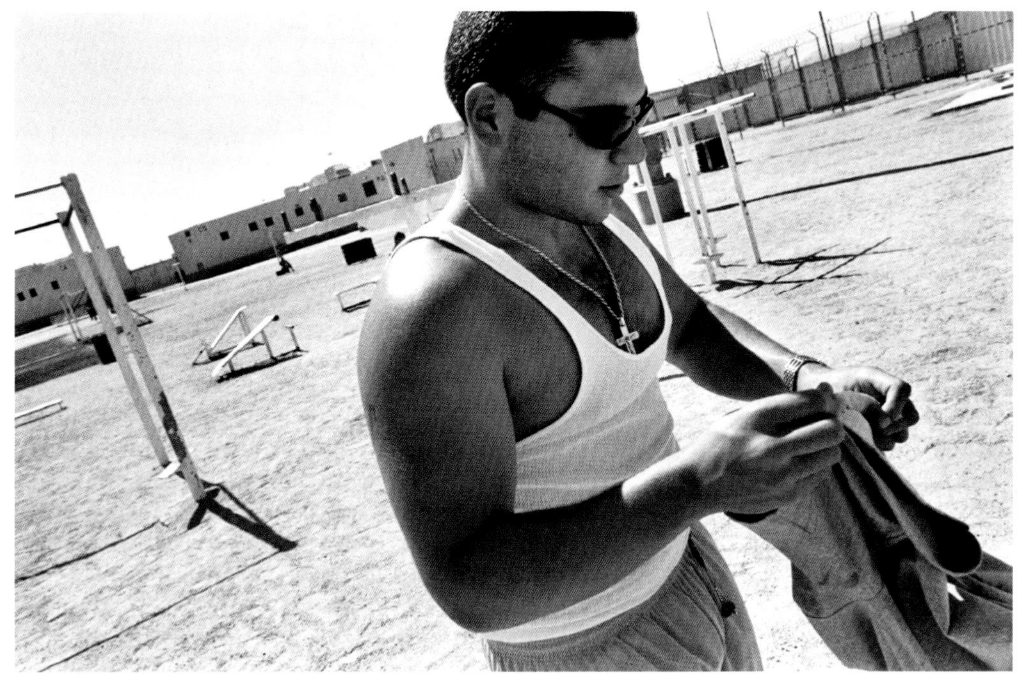

< In Between >

Heaven and hell,
Night and day,
Up and down.
Different in their own way,
But connected.
Send me to heaven,
But I don't deserve it.
Send me to hell,
I don't deserve that either.
Make an exeption and send me somewhere,
Because no one deserves this kind of life.

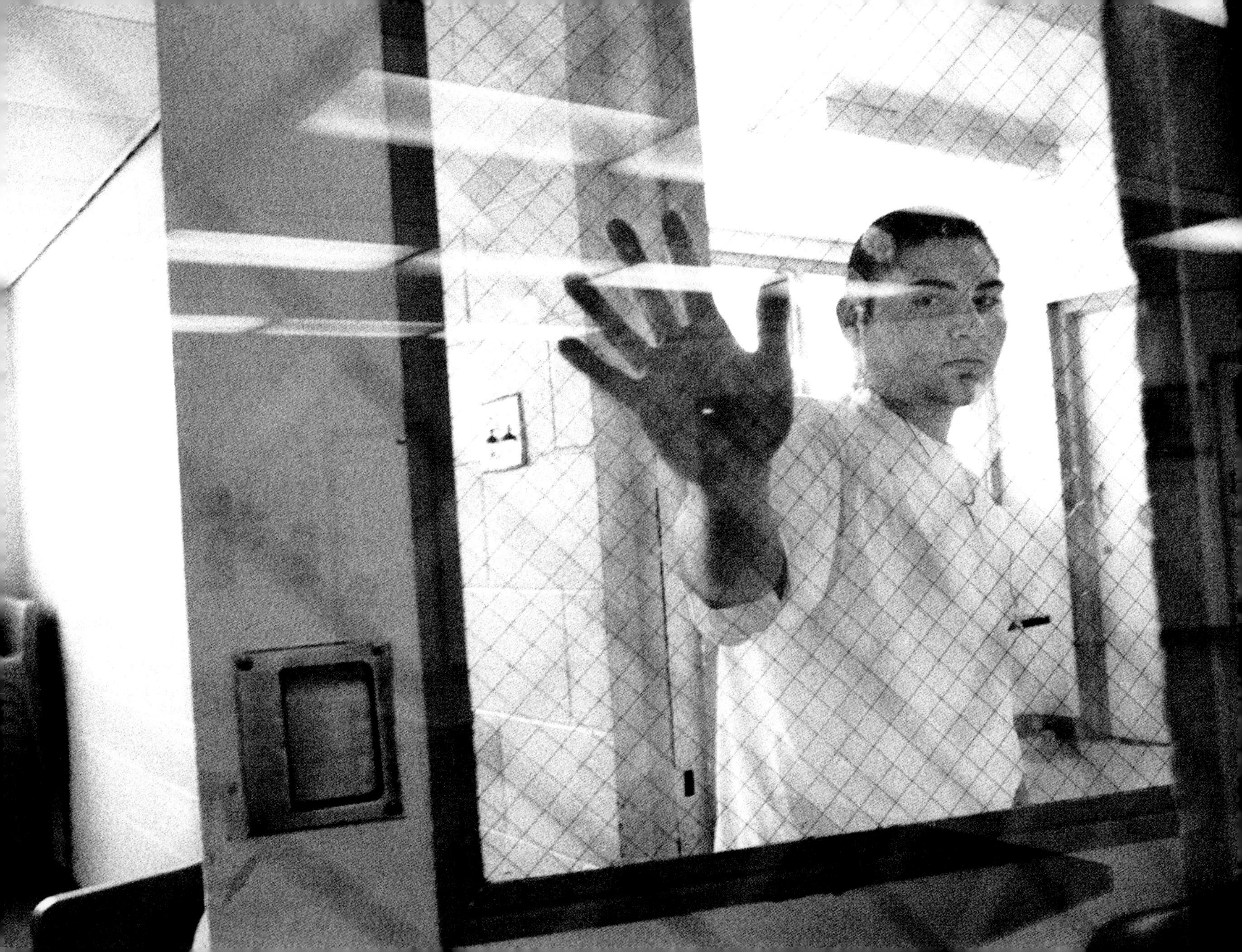

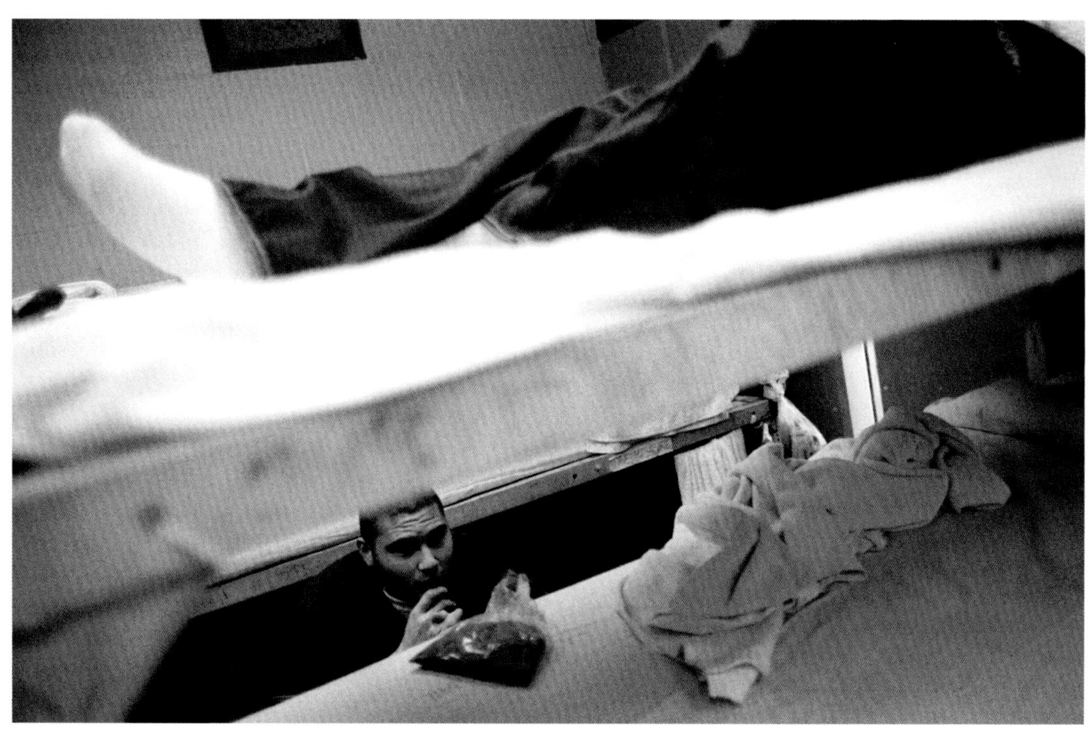

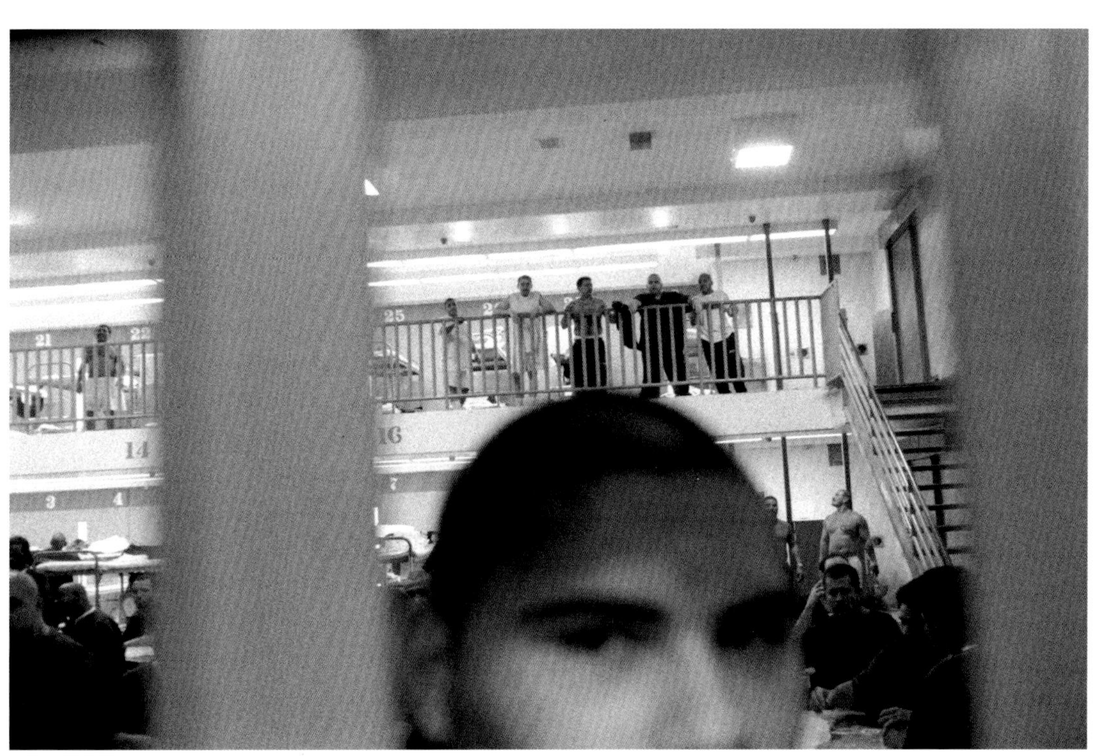

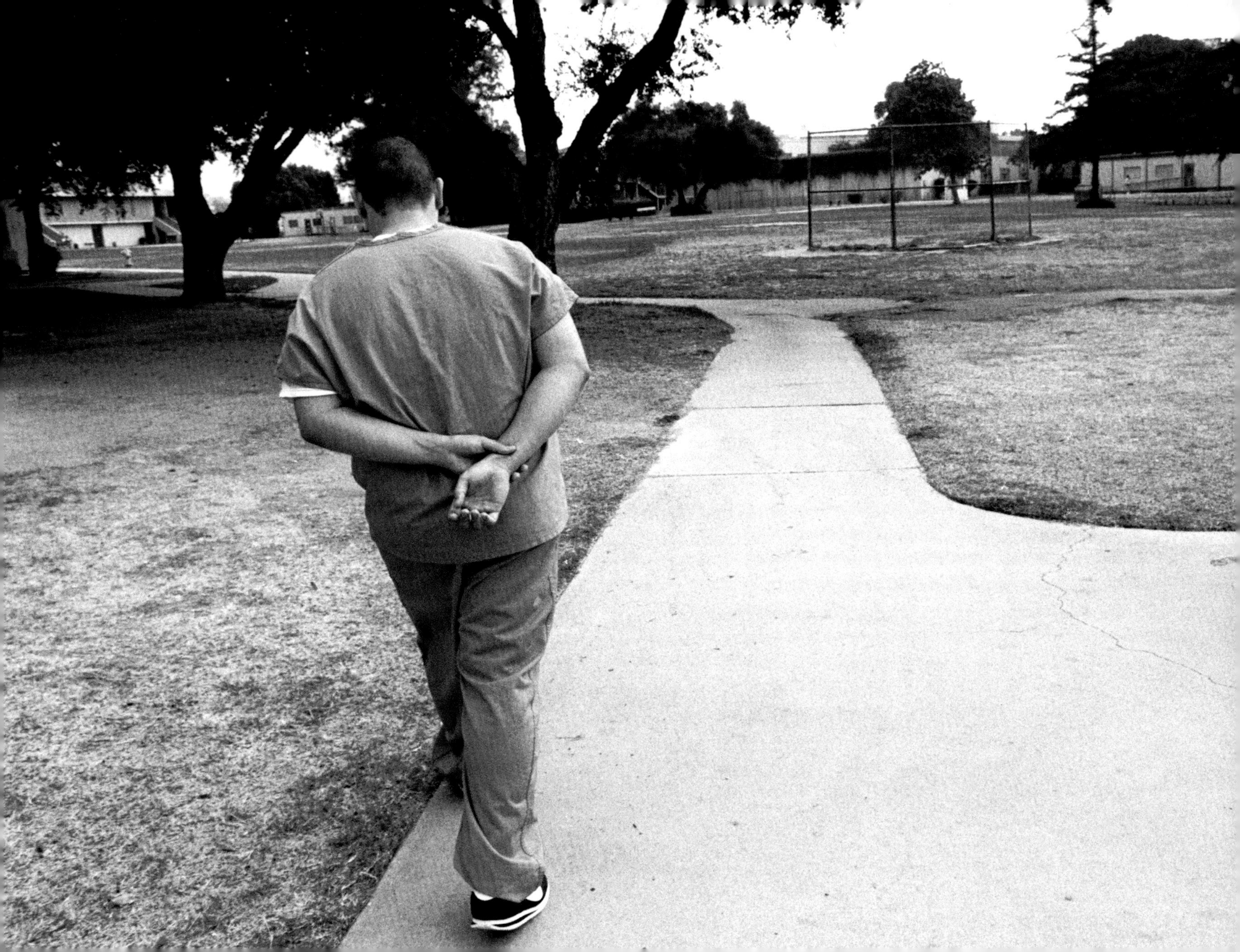

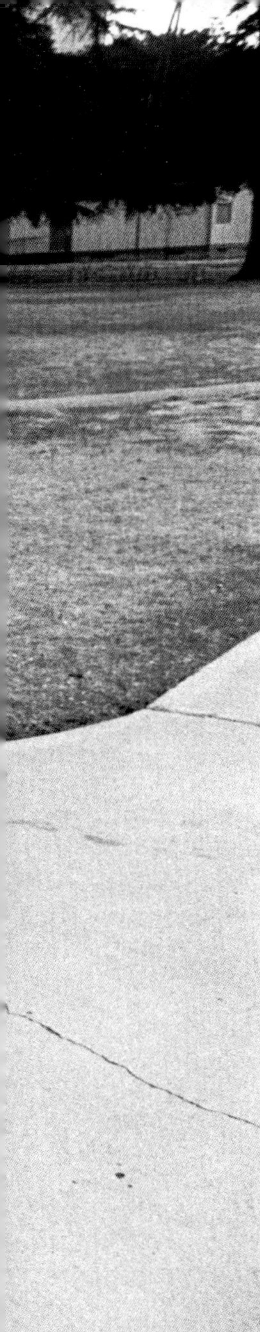

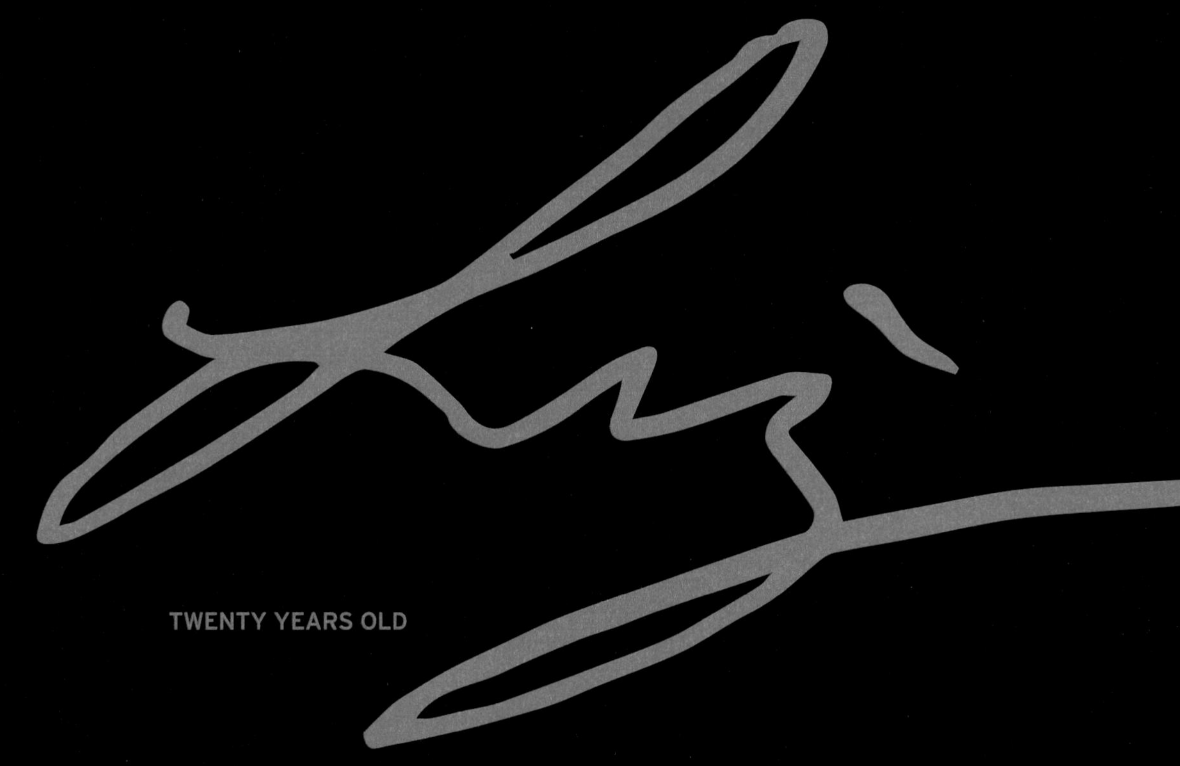
TWENTY YEARS OLD

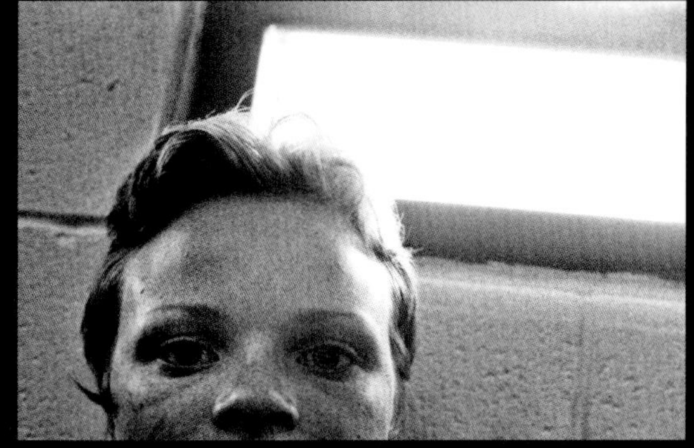

Liz was sexually abused by her stepfather from the age of nine, and was a runaway. She had been living on the streets for five years before her arrest at the age of fifteen-and-a-half. She was charged with accessory to murder for being present during the strangulation of a teenage woman in an abandoned building. Liz was sentenced to eleven years in adult prison. It was her first offense.

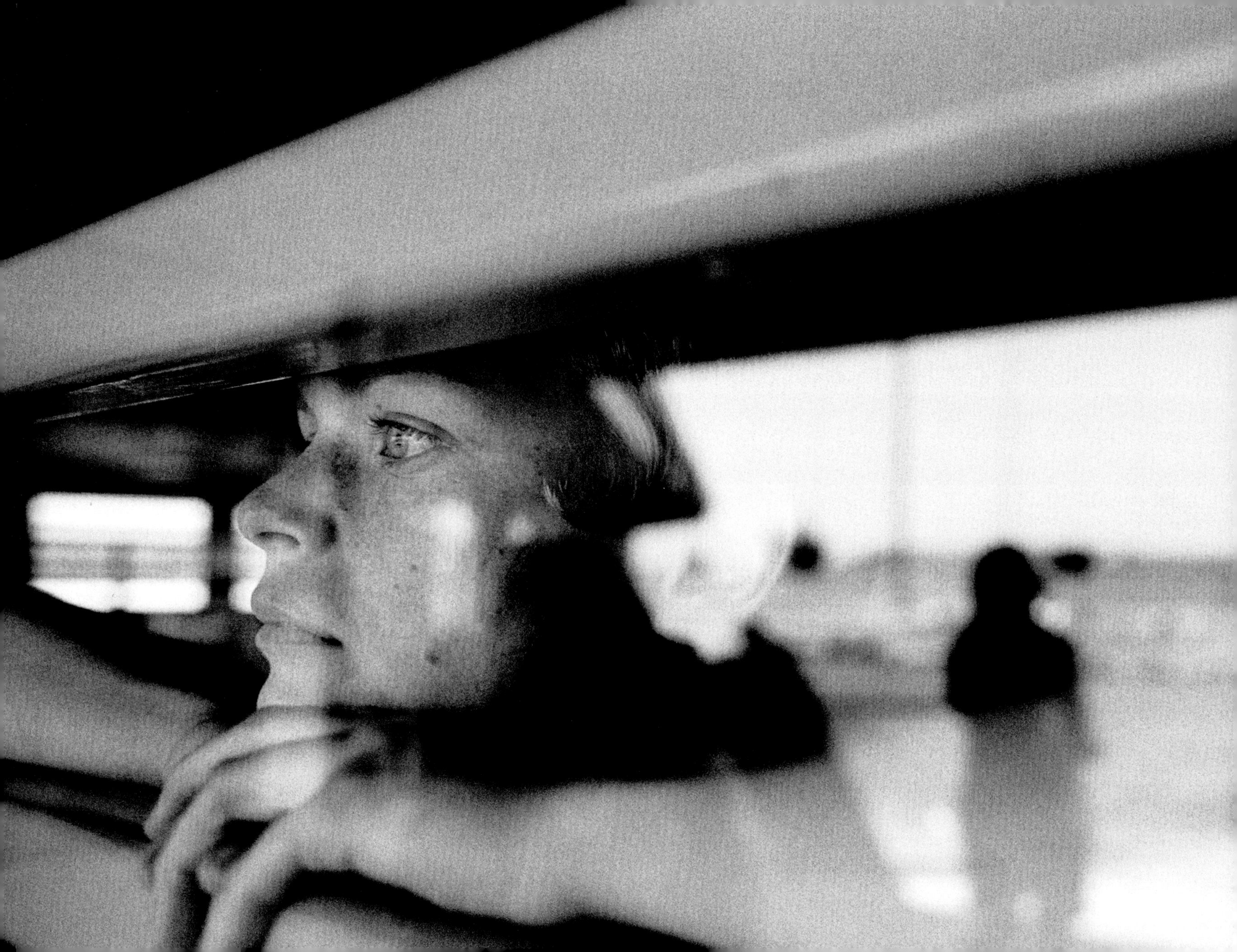

What com

What kind of

When has anyt

When the days

and we exist

of death.

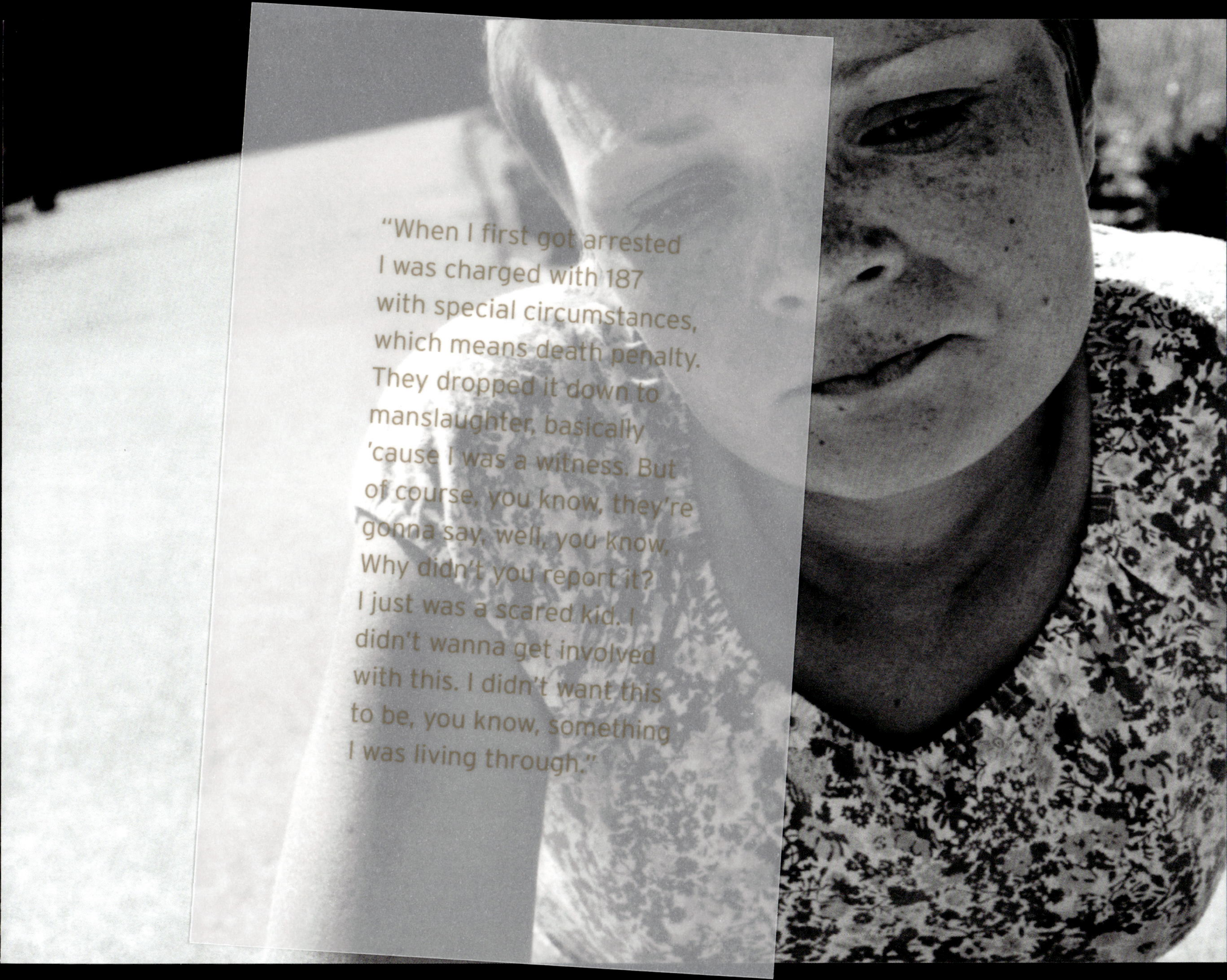

"When I first got arrested
I was charged with 187
with special circumstances,
which means death penalty.
They dropped it down to
manslaughter, basically
'cause I was a witness. But
of course, you know, they're
gonna say, well, you know,
Why didn't you report it?
I just was a scared kid. I
didn't wanna get involved
with this. I didn't want this
to be, you know, something
I was living through."

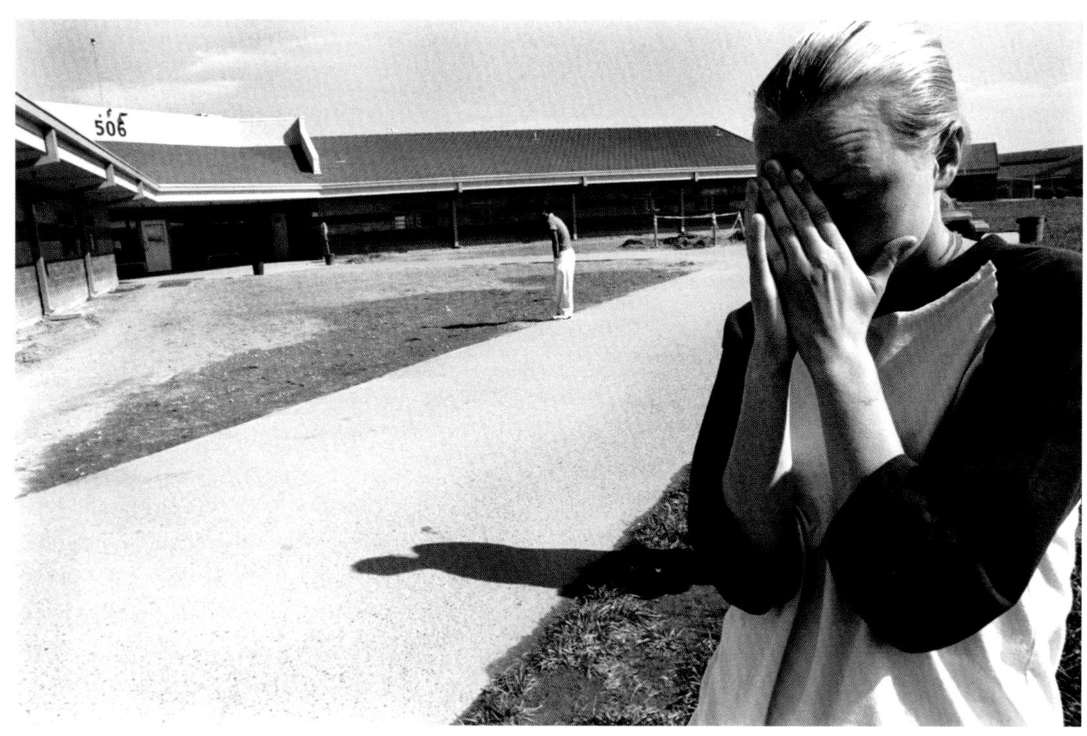

506

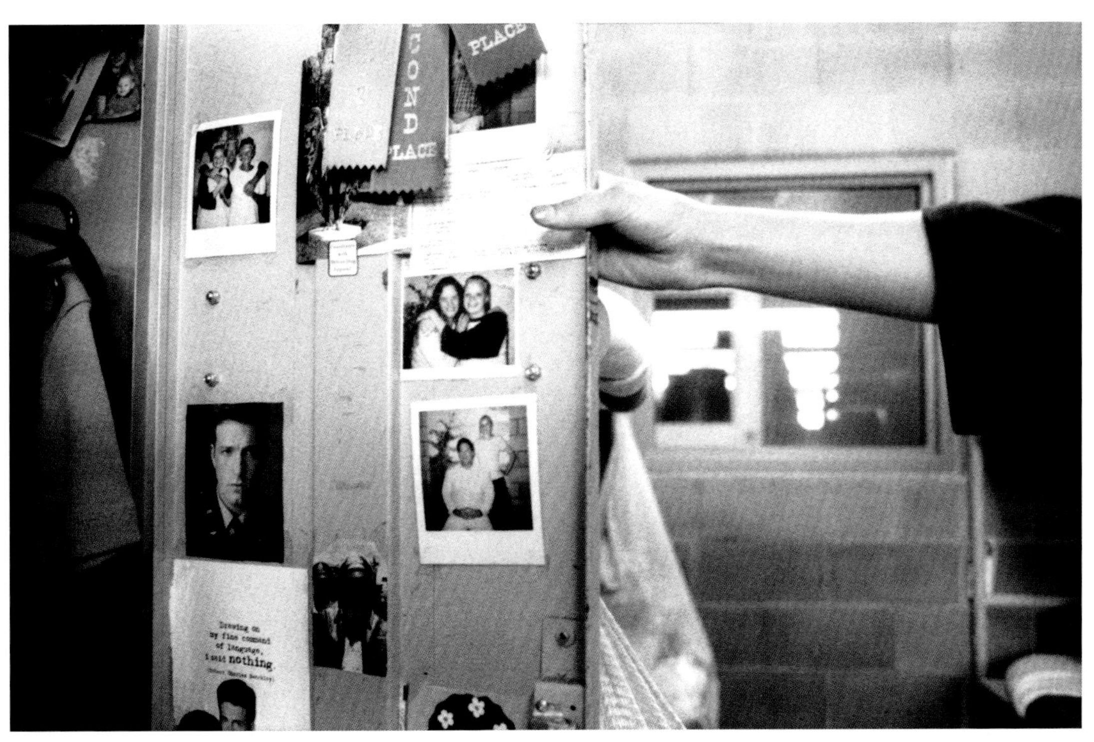

I am expected to fail.
they are counting on it
they are banking on it
trading stocks and investing on it.
My pain
My hurt
My future is appraised

and then

Auctioned on The Block.

506

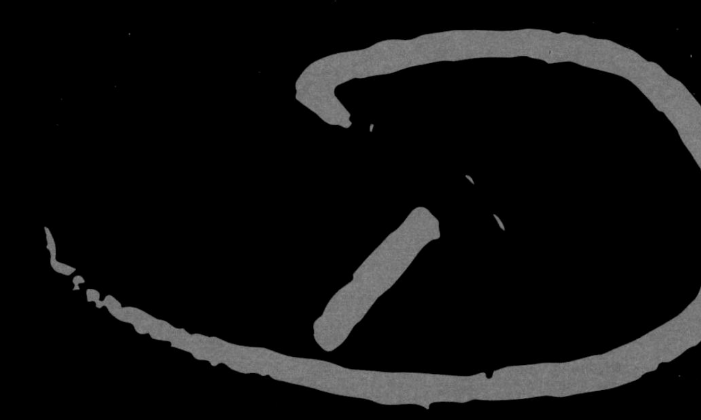

NINETEEN YEARS OLD

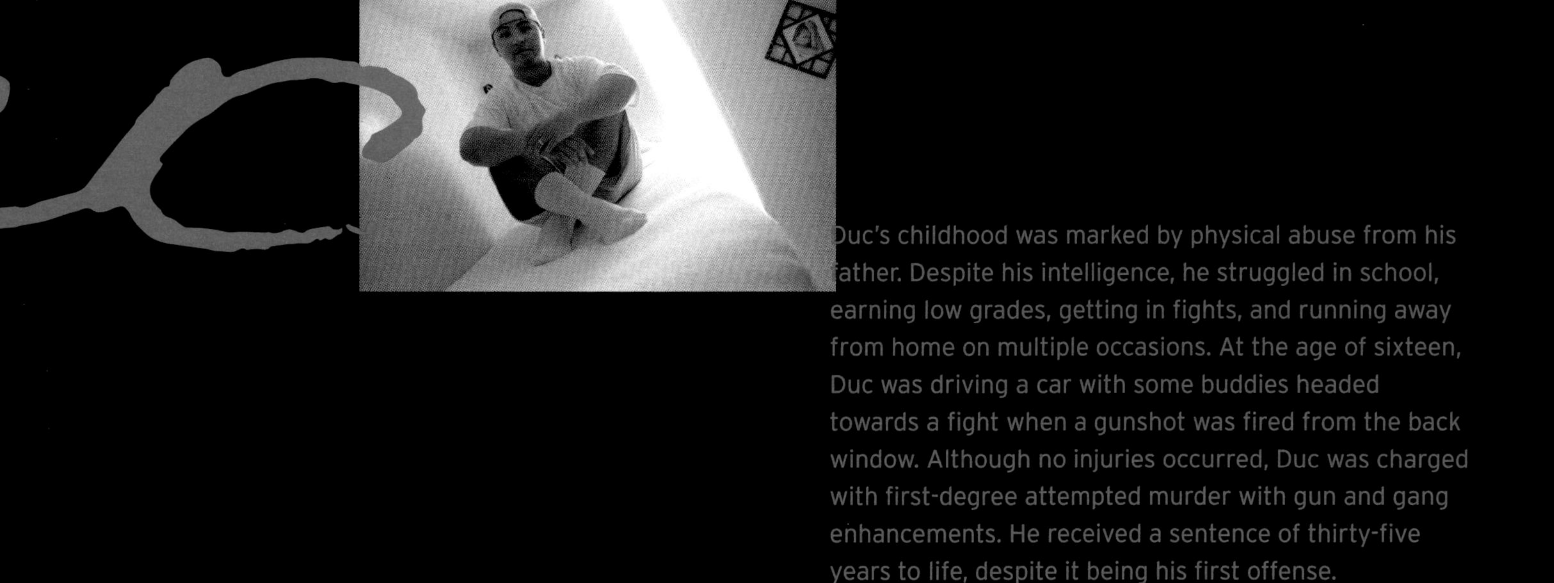

Duc's childhood was marked by physical abuse from his father. Despite his intelligence, he struggled in school, earning low grades, getting in fights, and running away from home on multiple occasions. At the age of sixteen, Duc was driving a car with some buddies headed towards a fight when a gunshot was fired from the back window. Although no injuries occurred, Duc was charged with first-degree attempted murder with gun and gang enhancements. He received a sentence of thirty-five years to life, despite it being his first offense.

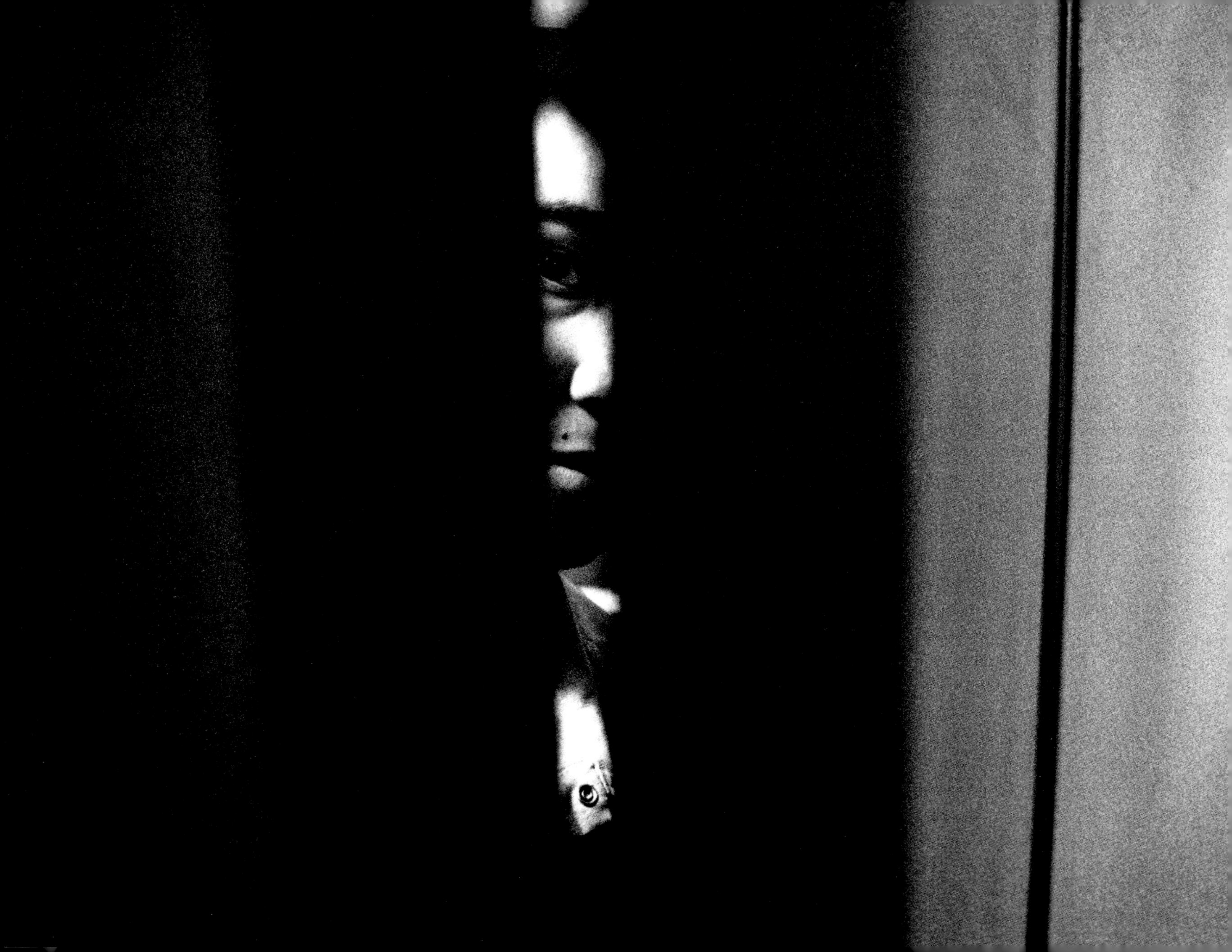

Trapped inside a shell
That won't hatch.
Trying to break free
And start the new me.

I found the new me.
How? Well, let me tell you.
People and friends who
Believed. Believed not
Only in me, but in humanity.

Showed me things I
Would never see or even believe.
But they did, and
By that I am mentally Free.

The physical part
I'm gonna just have
To wait and see.

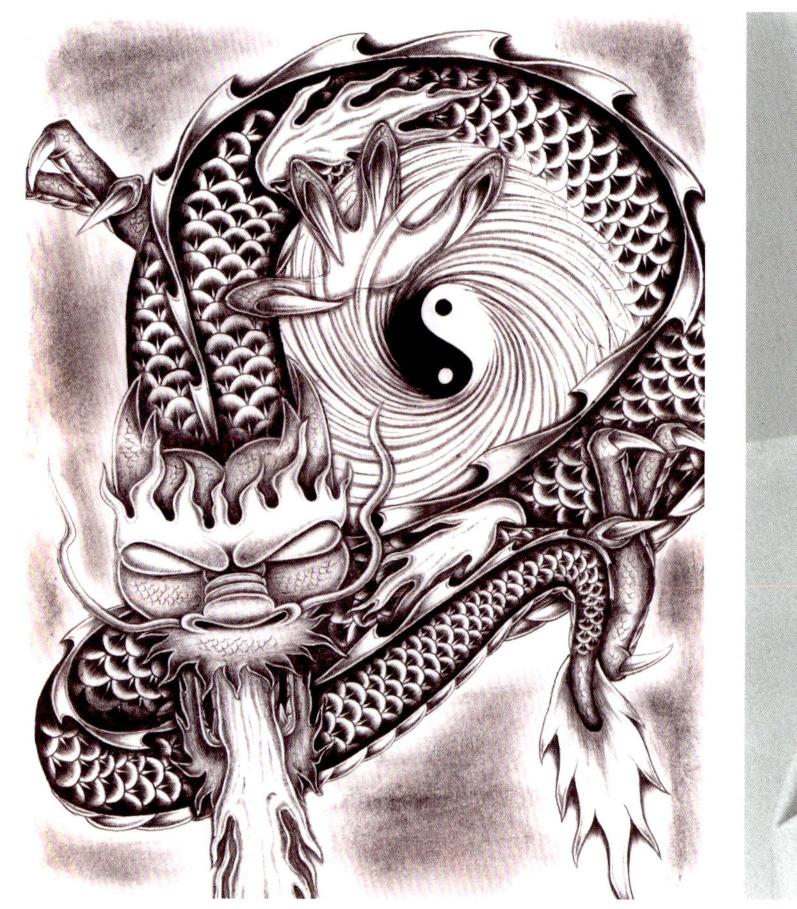

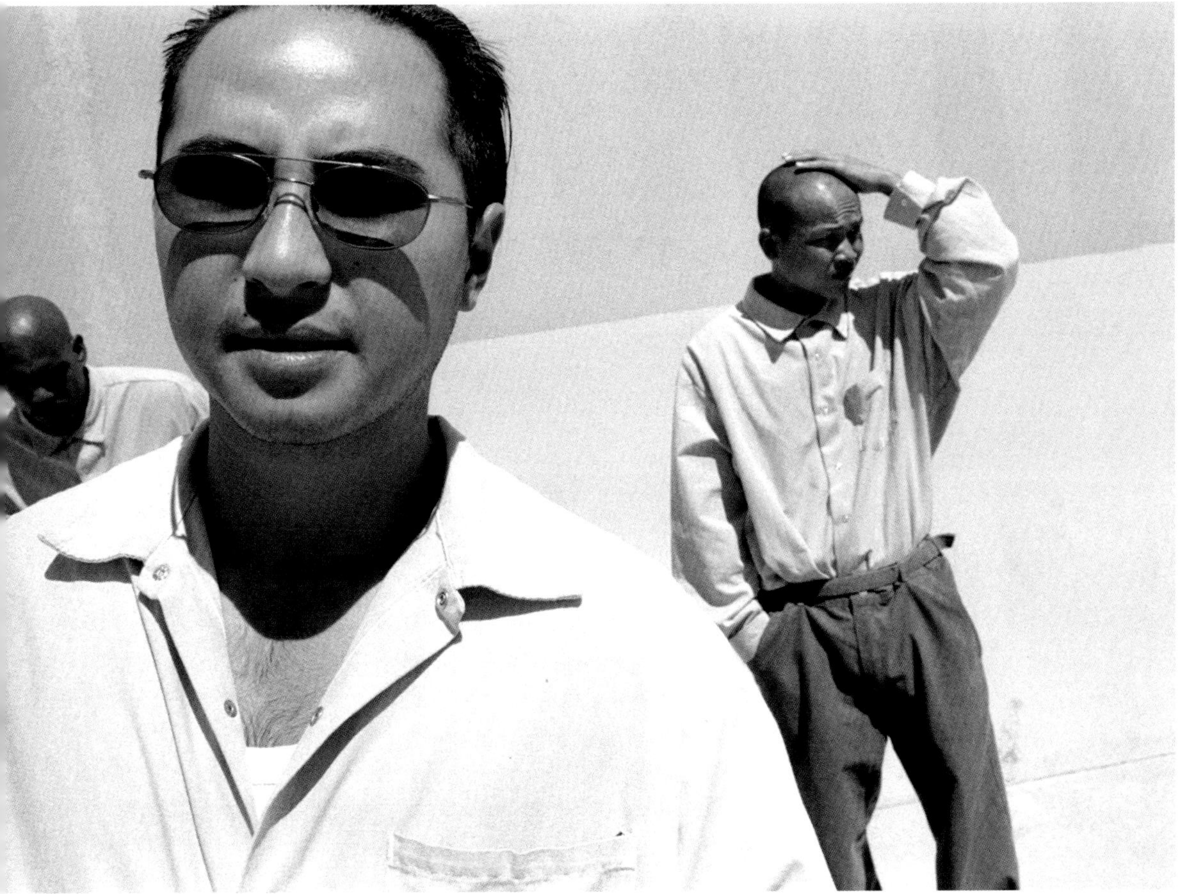

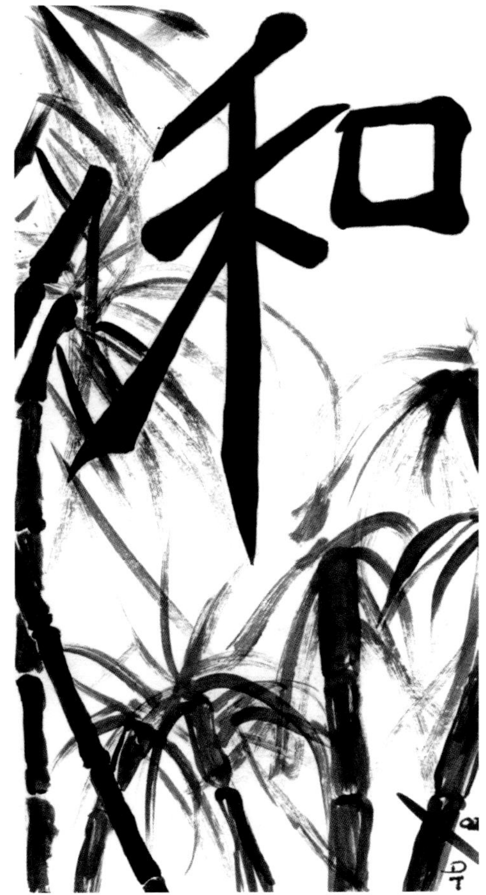

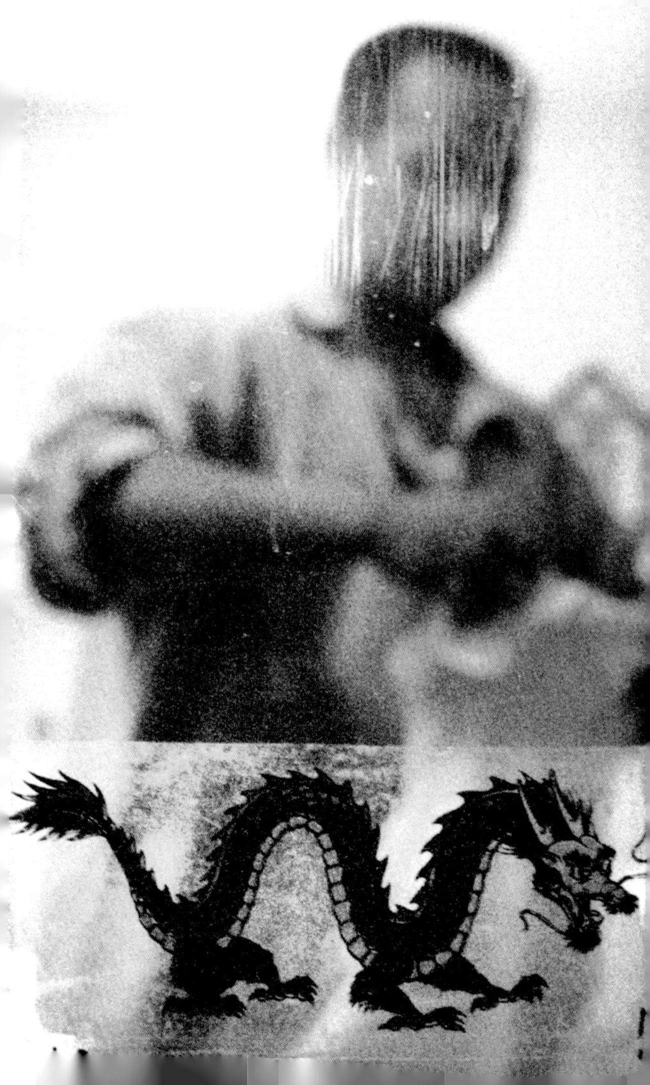

"In first grade, I got in a fight
with one of my classmates
and my parents had to come
down and take me out of
school. [They take] me home,
just, you know, go inside the
house. It's just, just wait for
him [my father]. You know,
he'd get whatever he can get
to hit me with. You can't do
nothing. And after it hurt too
much, I can't lay still anymore,
I start to get up and I started
to run. He'll come after me.".

"In first grade, I got in a fight
with one of my classmates
and my parents had to come
down and take me out of
school. [They take] me home,
just, you know, go inside the
house. It's just, just wait for
him [my father]. You know,
he'd get whatever he can get
to hit me with. You can't do
nothing. And after it hurt too
much, I can't lay still anymore,
I start to get up and I started
to run. He'll come after me."

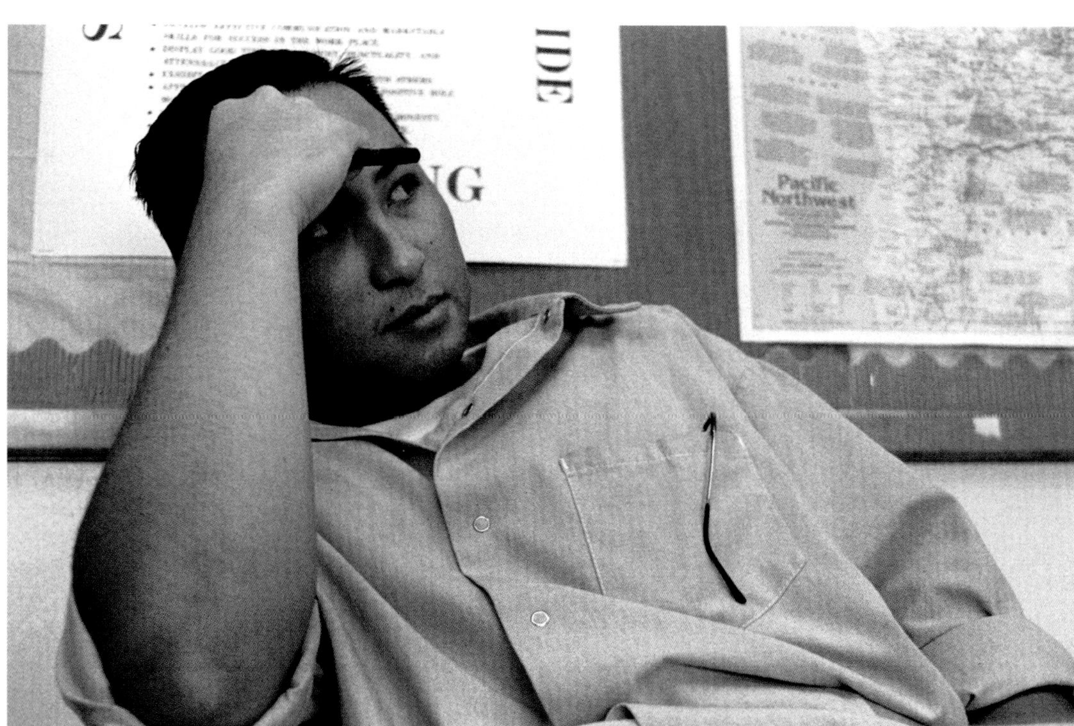

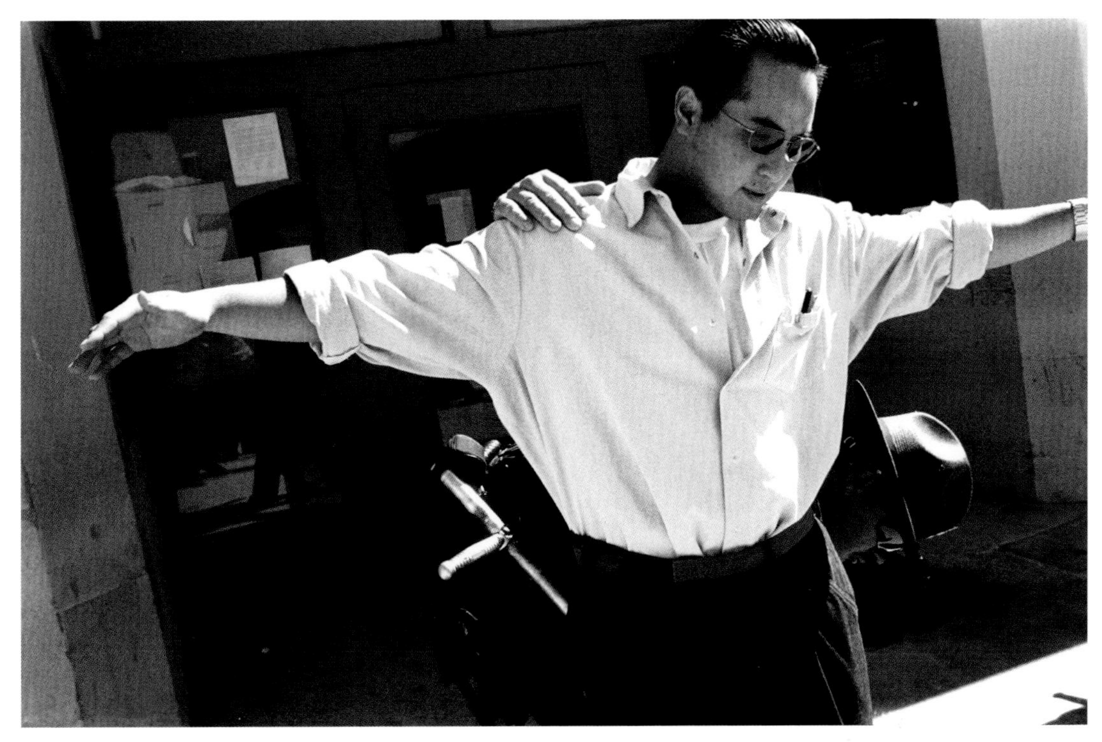

Two Lives to live
But just one man
Stuck between good and bad
Slowly but surely going mad

First life is instinct
Just to stay alive
Stripped down and left to die
Prison rules is what he goes by

Second life is home
Where light surrounds his road
Just to be himself and free
Letting him become what he wants to be

But his first life
Gets him stuck deeper
He punches, kicks and screams
Still alone, left to survive by any means

Alone in a darkness of depression
His mind shifts around
Love, hate, anger and happiness
Left to think of the things he missed

He prays for the strength to hold on
For how long the answer is unknown
For what reason?
Hopefully, to make it through
another four seasons

Once again he has made it through
Another day of this life
But he knows hell will break loose again
Maybe tomorrow, next week,
who knows when

Two Lives to live
But just one man
Stuck between good and bad
Slowly but surely,
you think he'll go mad?

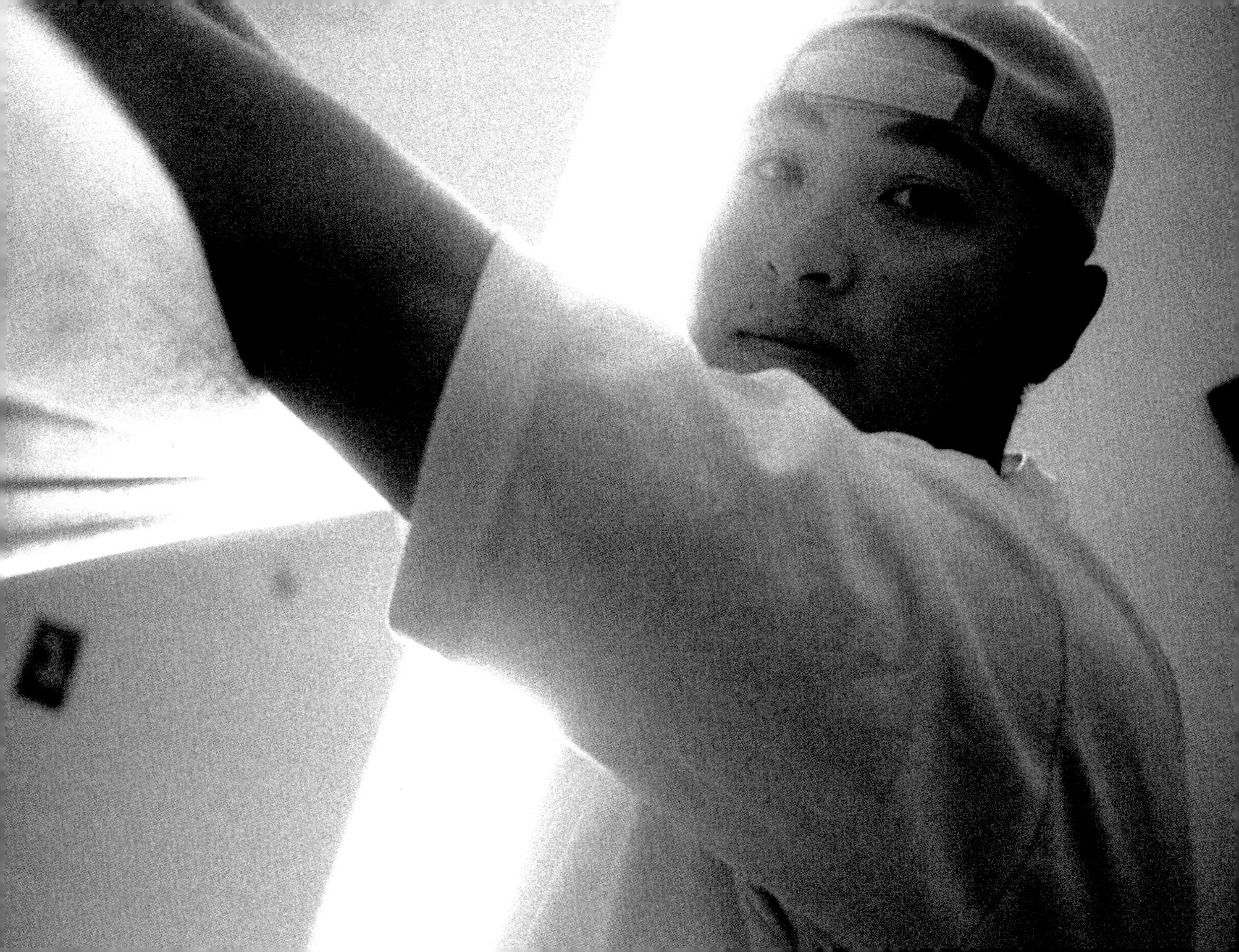

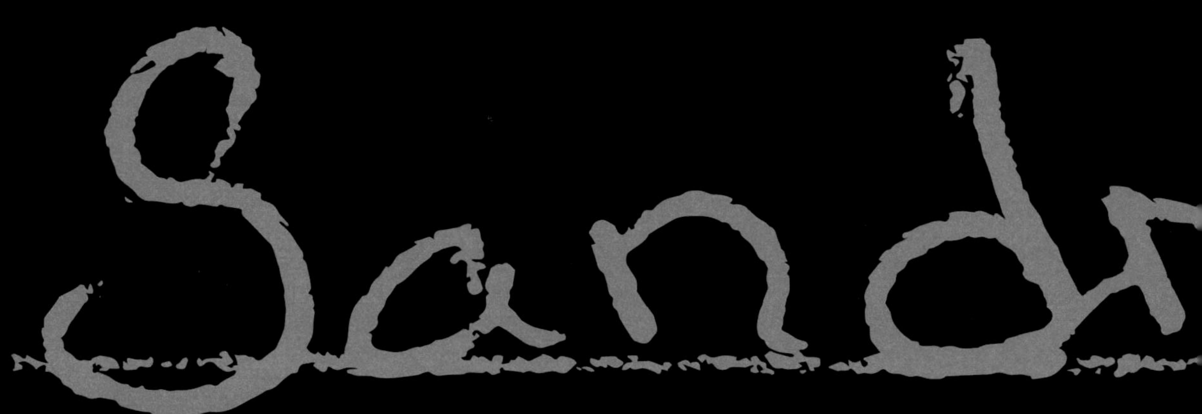

TWENTY YEARS OLD

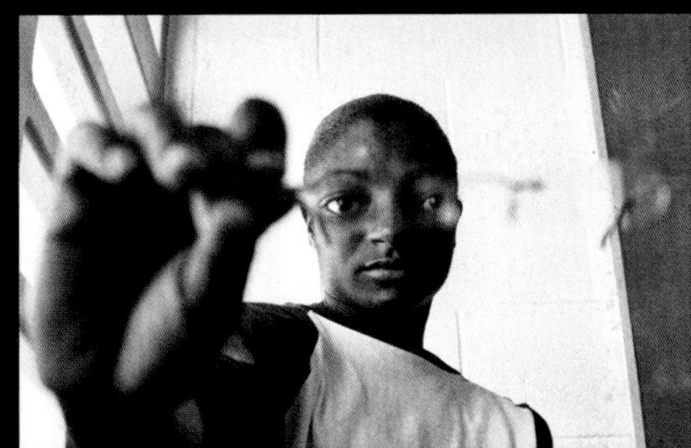

Sandra grew up without the presence of both parents. At the age of twelve, she was raped and became a single mother. Throughout her teenage years, Sandra lived as a runaway, evading child protective services. At seventeen, a phone card registered in her name was discovered at a murder scene, which led to her arrest on charges of being an accessory to murder. She was sentenced to twenty-seven years to life in adult prison. It was her first offense.

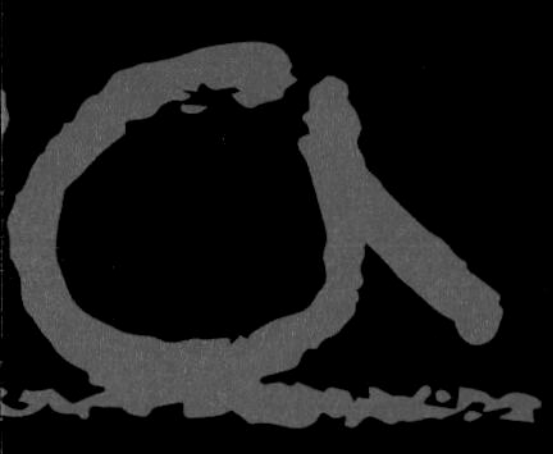

…use the

to feel

…and lonely.

…eight of the

…ad the

…all I

I don't

…se to go.

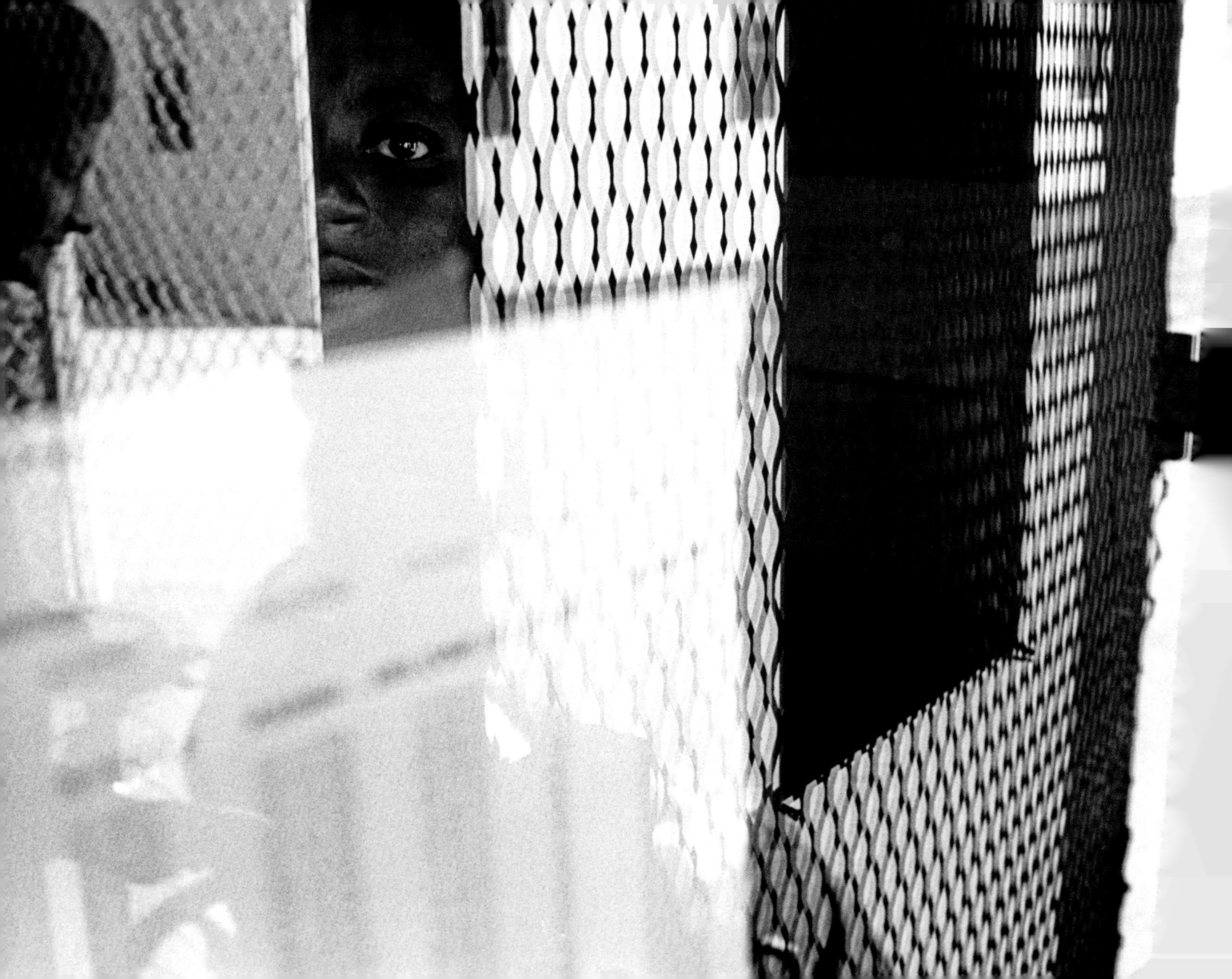

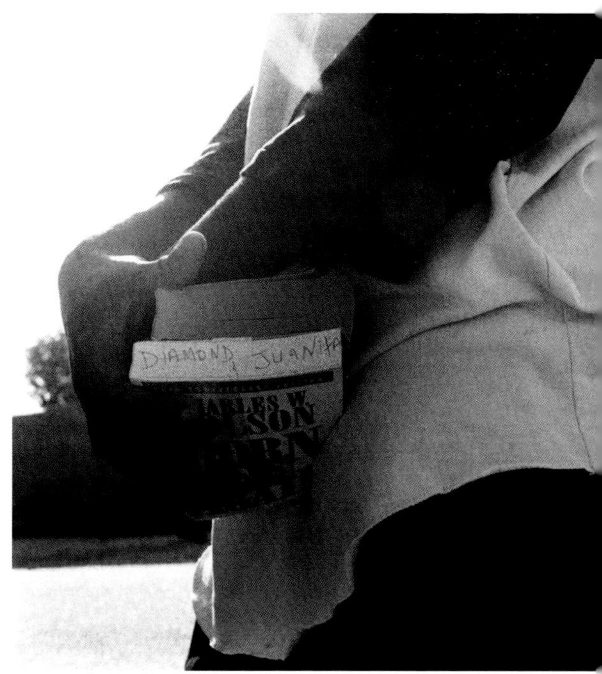
DIAMOND JUANITA

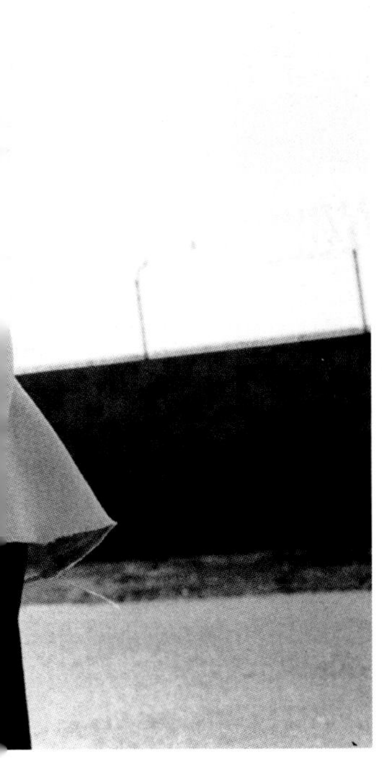
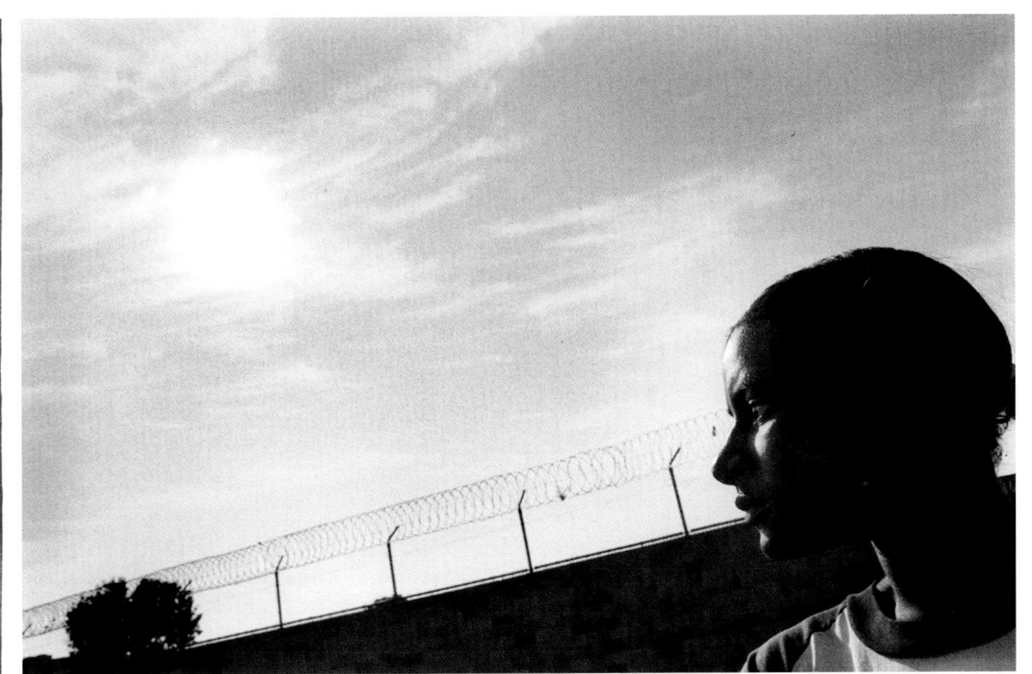

As for myself, every day here seems as though I'm on a roller-coaster-ride. One minute I feel great; high off life. Then depression hits me like a wild bull from behind. And I find myself struggling to regain breath.

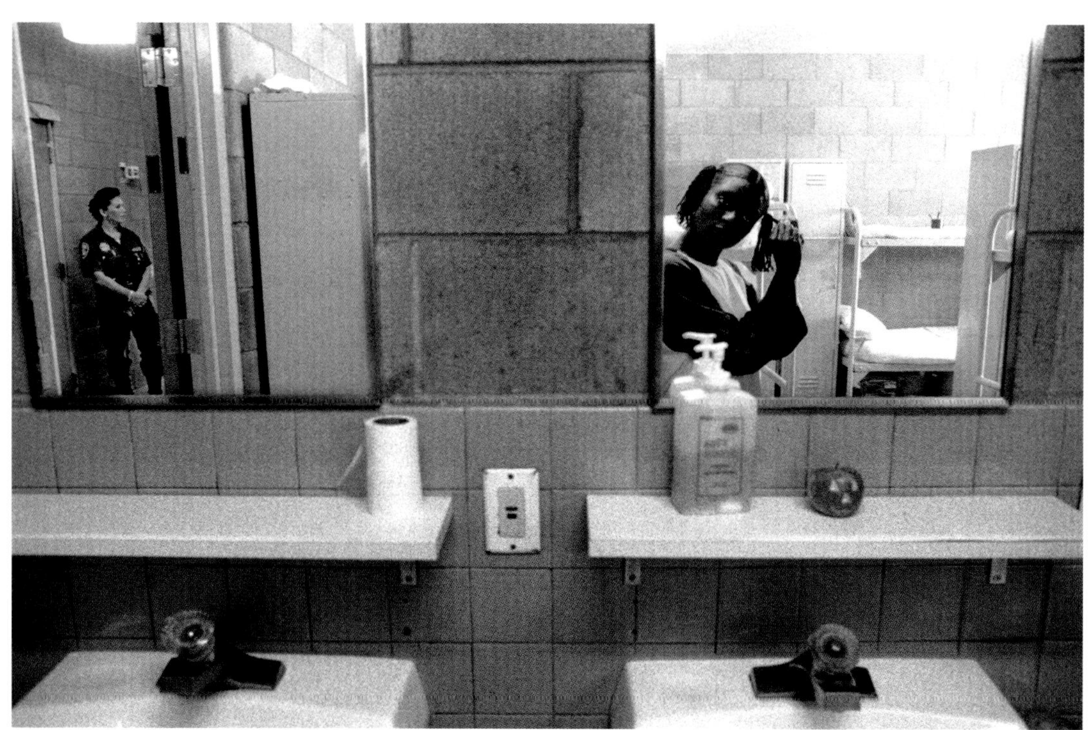

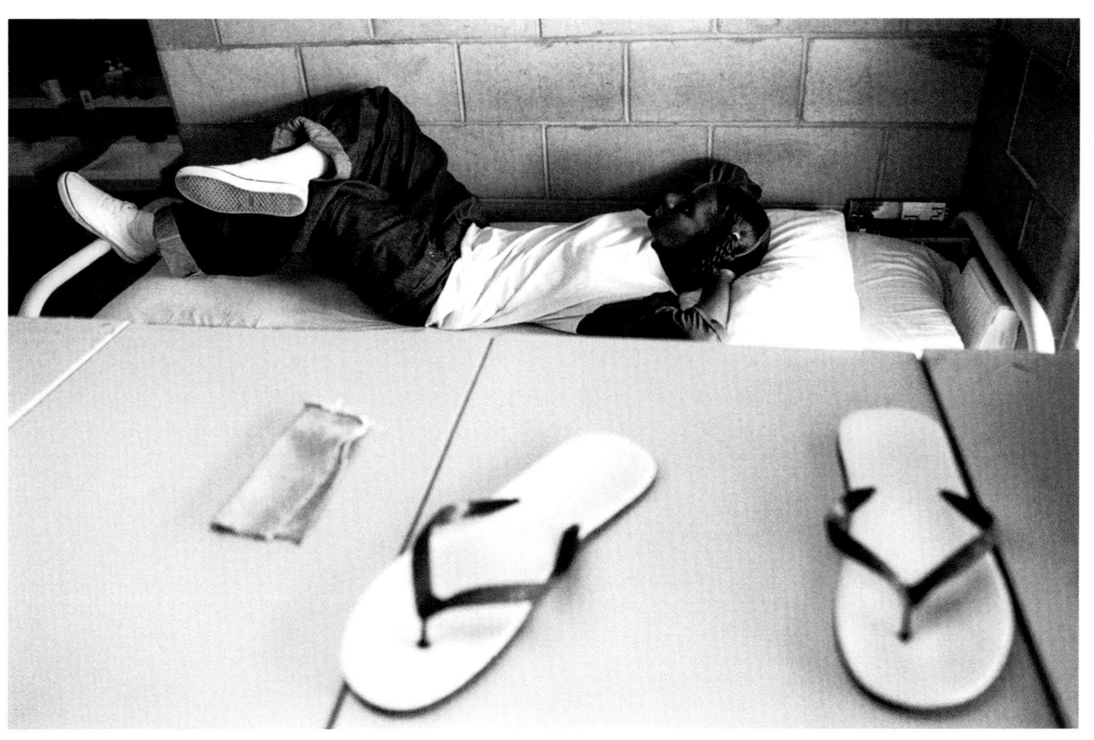

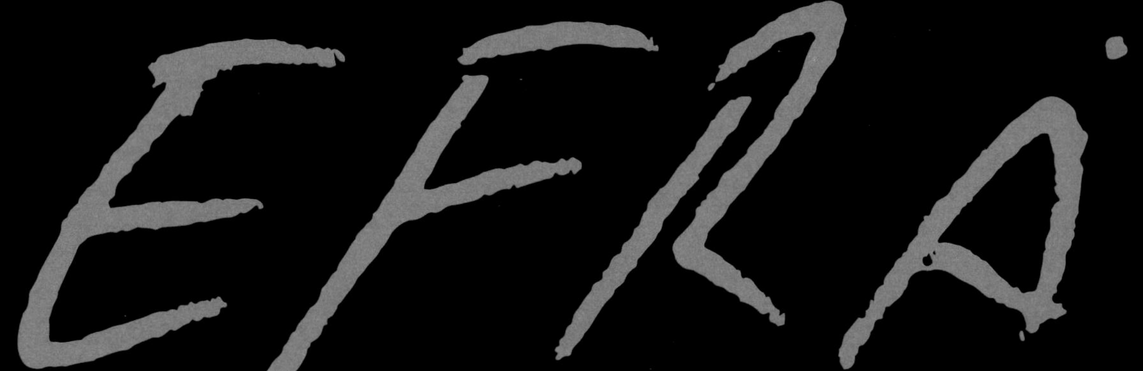
EFRA
EIGHTEEN YEARS OLD

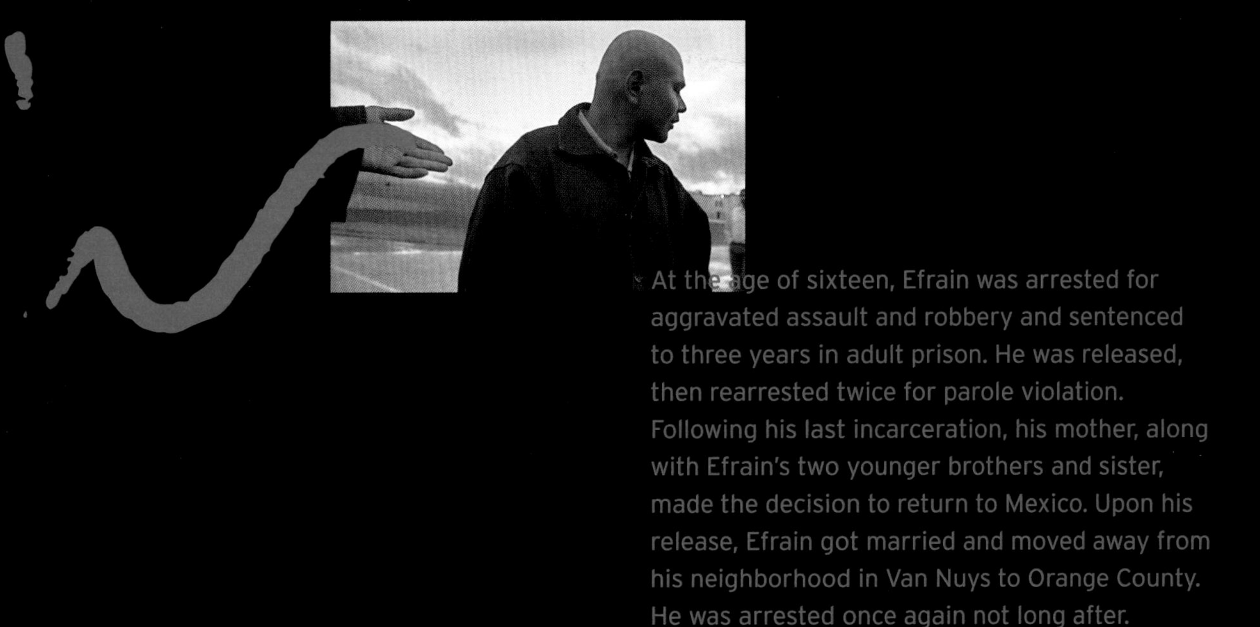

At the age of sixteen, Efrain was arrested for aggravated assault and robbery and sentenced to three years in adult prison. He was released, then rearrested twice for parole violation. Following his last incarceration, his mother, along with Efrain's two younger brothers and sister, made the decision to return to Mexico. Upon his release, Efrain got married and moved away from his neighborhood in Van Nuys to Orange County. He was arrested once again not long after.

FEAR

FEAR IS seeing Him
FEAR IS being next to Him
FEAR IS calling Him for Help
I FEAR Him
I dont trust Him
I miss Him
My tHoughts scare me
My lIFE I owe to Him
MY INCARSARATION I owe to Him
FEAR IS seeing Him
FEAR IS being next to Him
FEAR IS Asking Him for Help
FEAR IS calling Him DAD

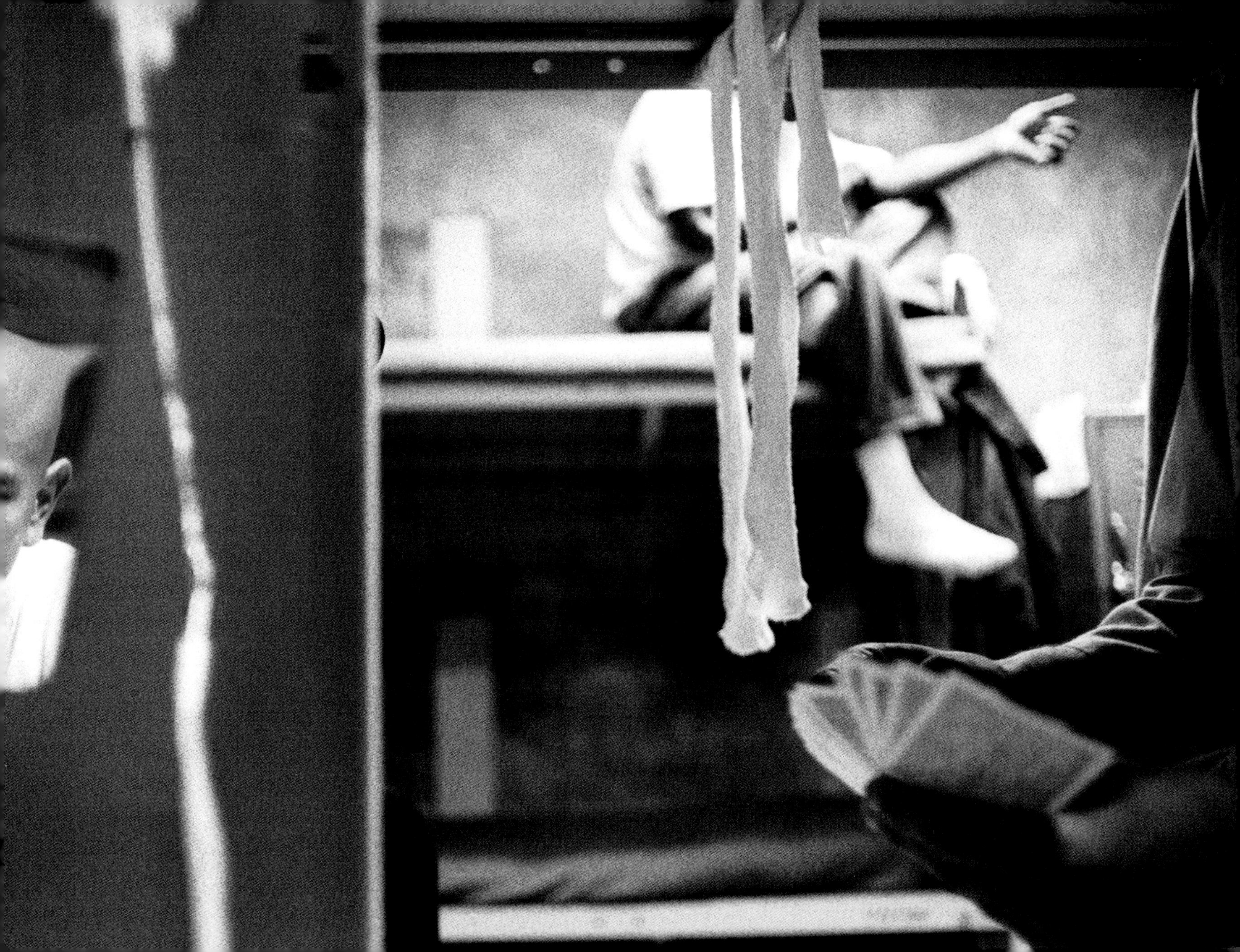

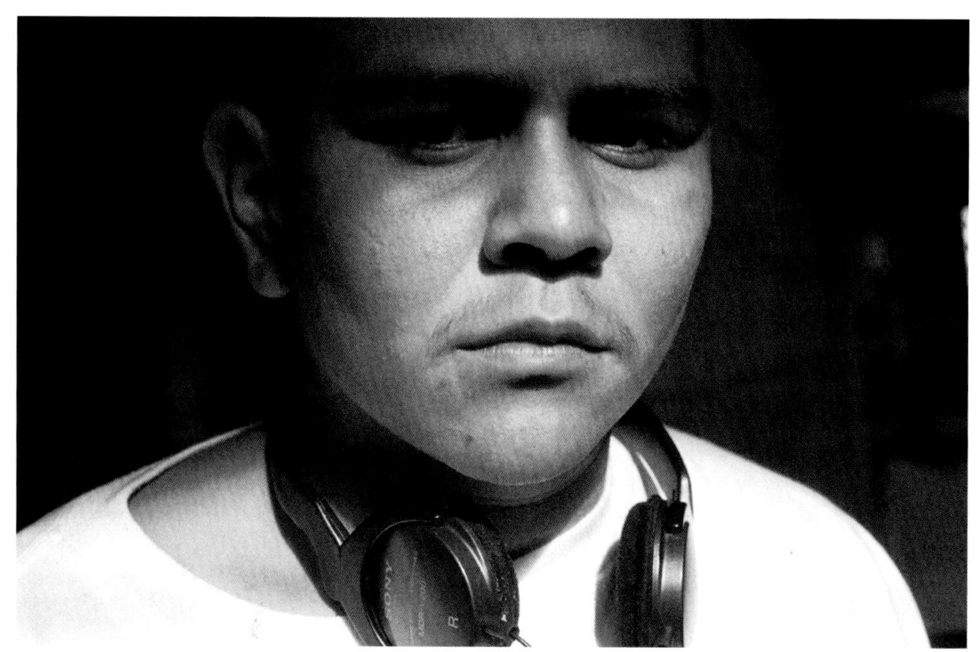

"And I get the bag and it says
'Avenal' on it. So then we get
here and the first person I
see is my dad. We won't be
getting high together, you
know what I mean? We won't
be doing certain things, won't
have any distractions. Maybe
we can just sit down and have
conversations from here. And,
you know what I mean? I'm
gonna lose four years of my
life and whatnot, but the way
I look at it, I got to know who
my dad really was."

"And I get the bag and it says 'Avenal' on it. So then we get here and the first person I see is my dad. We won't be getting high together, you know what I mean? We won't be doing certain things, won't have any distractions. Maybe we can just sit down and have conversations from here. And, you know what I mean? I'm gonna lose four years of my life and whatnot, but the way I look at it, I got to know who my dad really was."

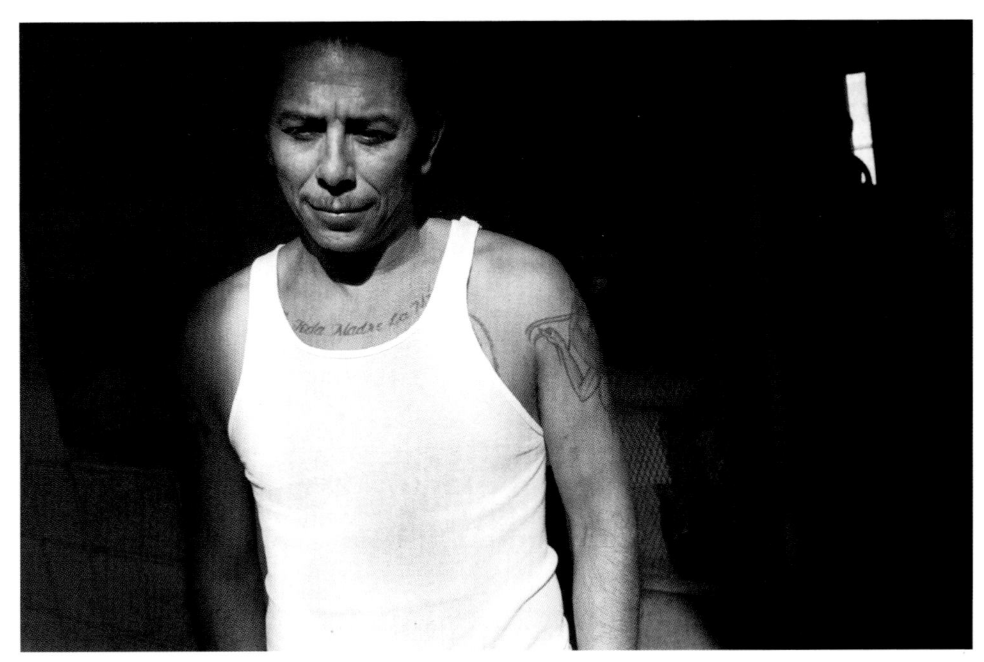

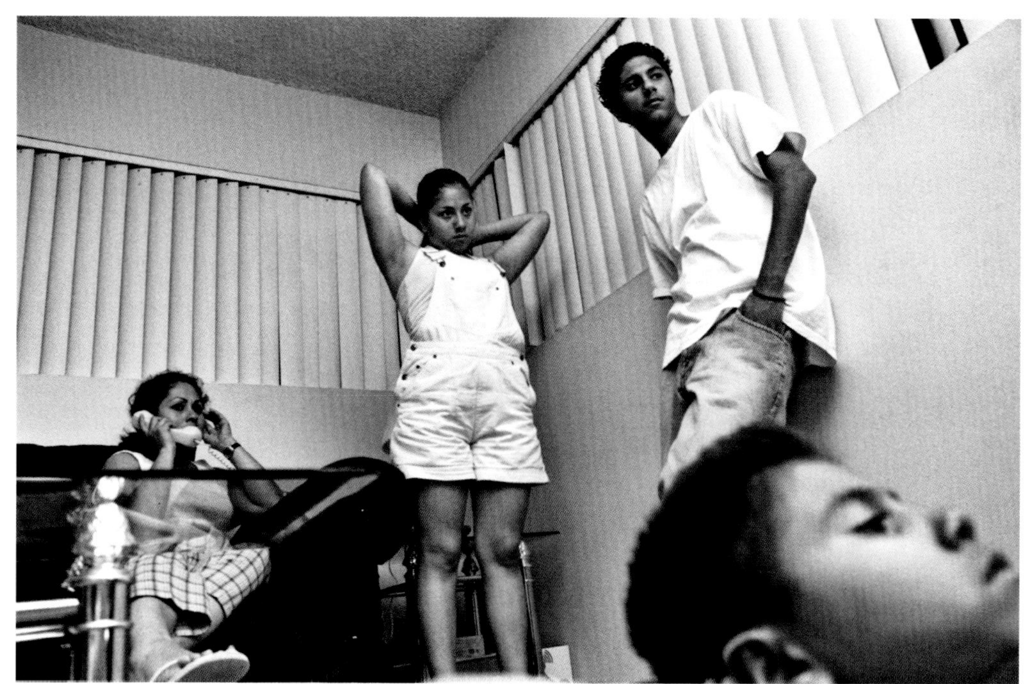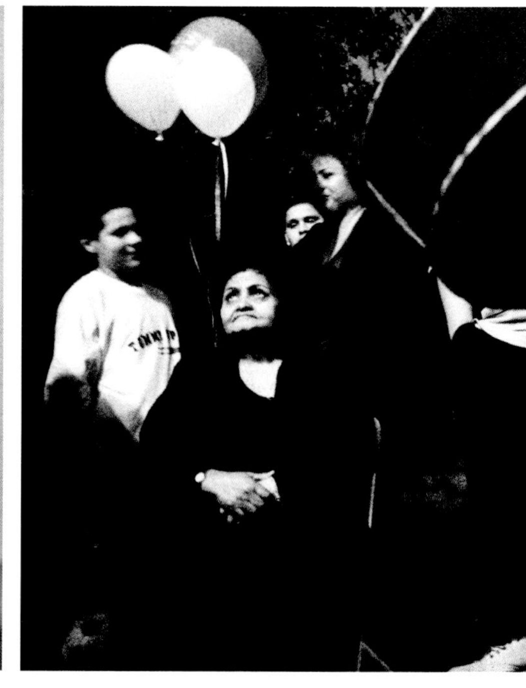

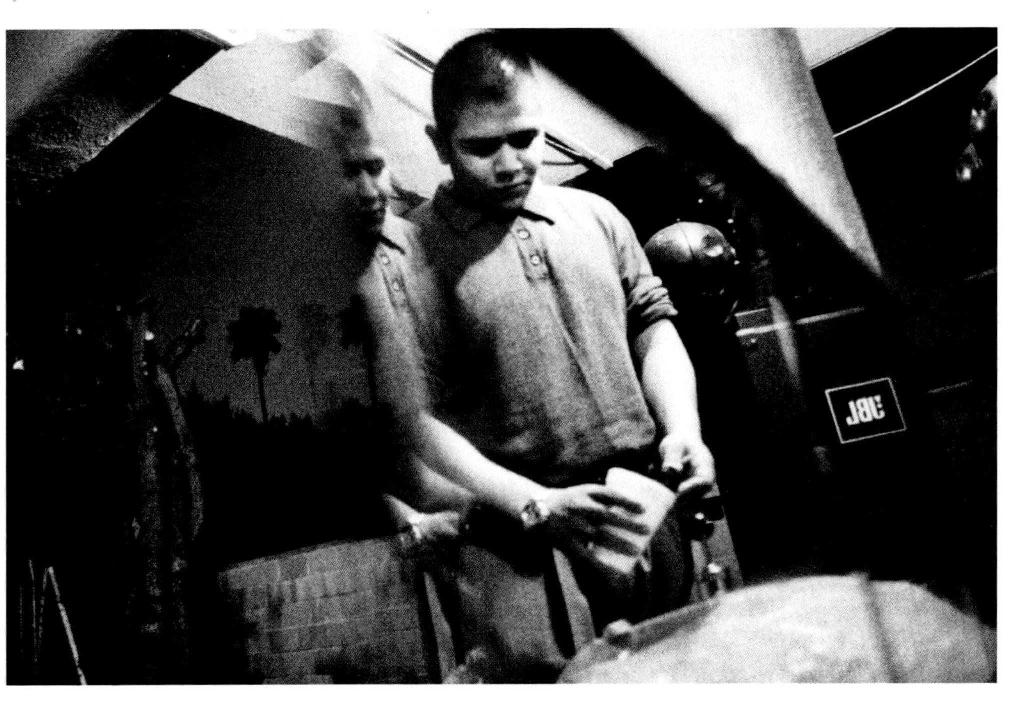

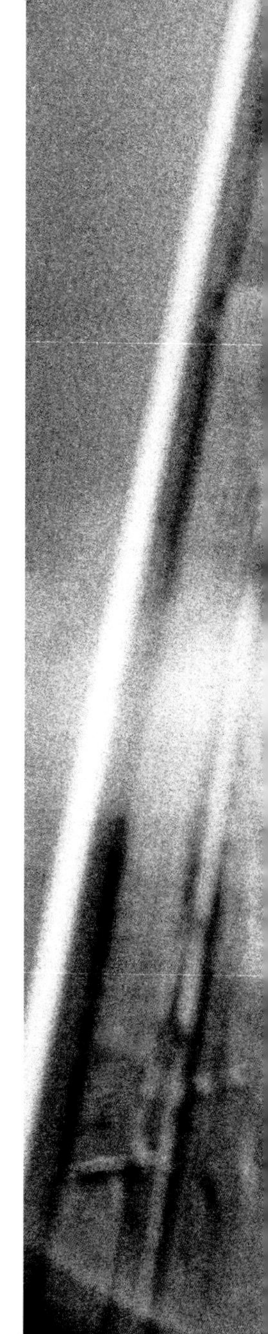

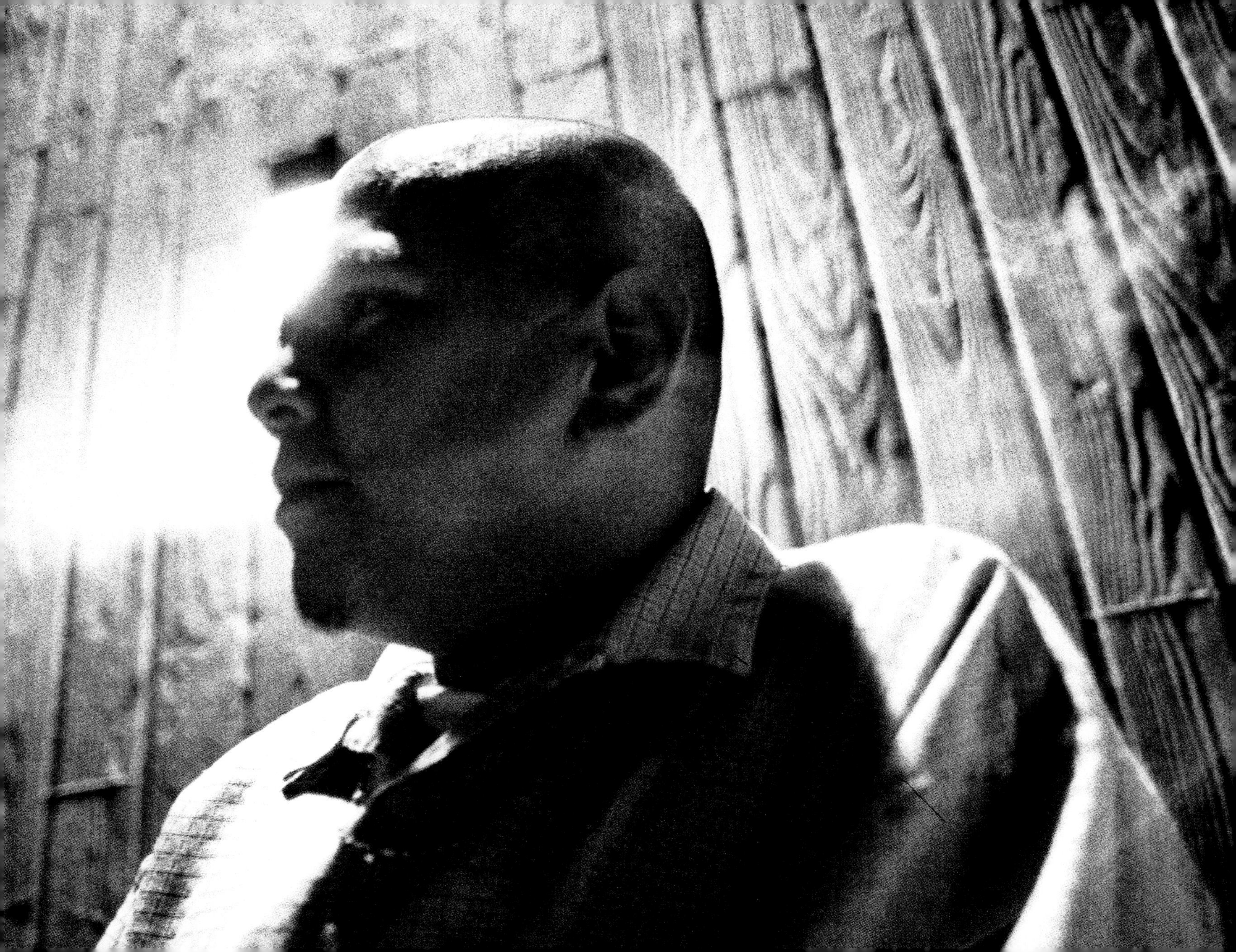

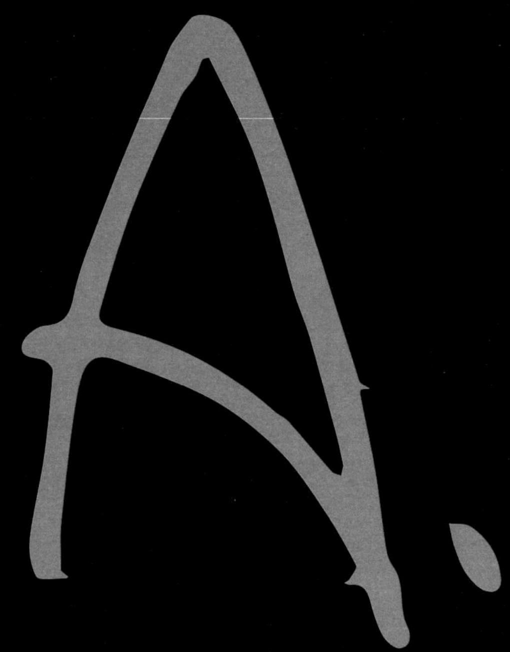
SIXTEEN YEARS OLD

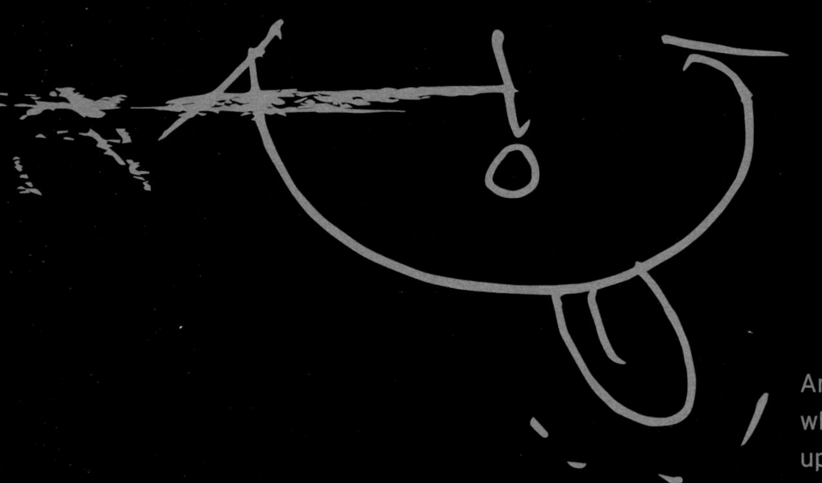

Anait's family immigrated to the United States when she was just four years old. Growing up as an only child, she was a good student and had a lot of freedom at home. At the age of fourteen, Anait was arrested for driving school friends to a fight where an innocent bystander was fatally stabbed. She became the youngest juvenile in California's history to be tried as an adult. Despite it being her first offense, Anait faced a severe charge of first-degree murder and was ultimately sentenced to seven years in prison.

I cant
be getting into any trouble
but I cant help it I guess
Im always in trouble I was
on lock down on The 25th. for
x-mas on the 26. I just got
sent to my Room today for
using a lot of profanity
I just need to get out
jail is getting to me.
I think Im going crazy
I'm 17 years old now

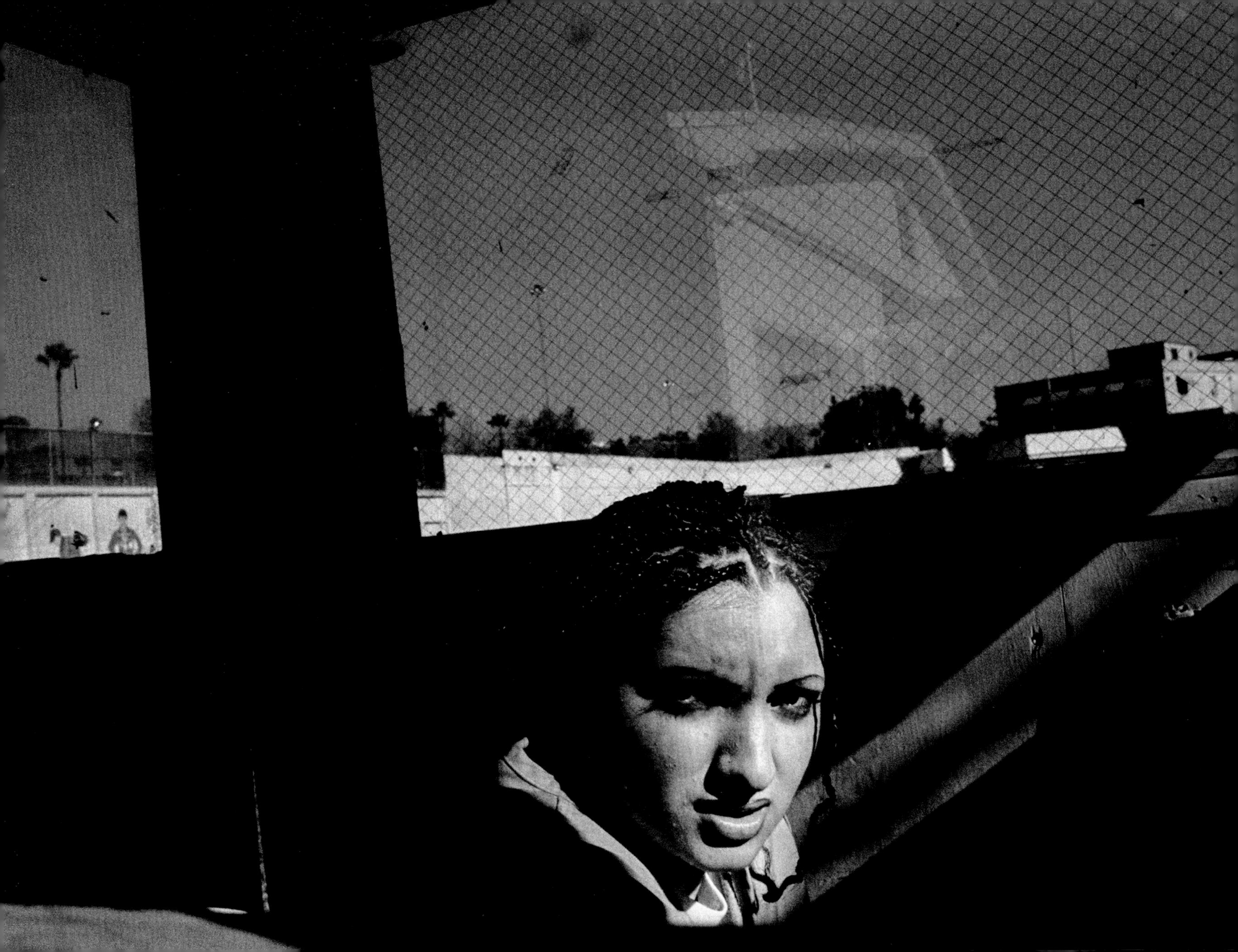

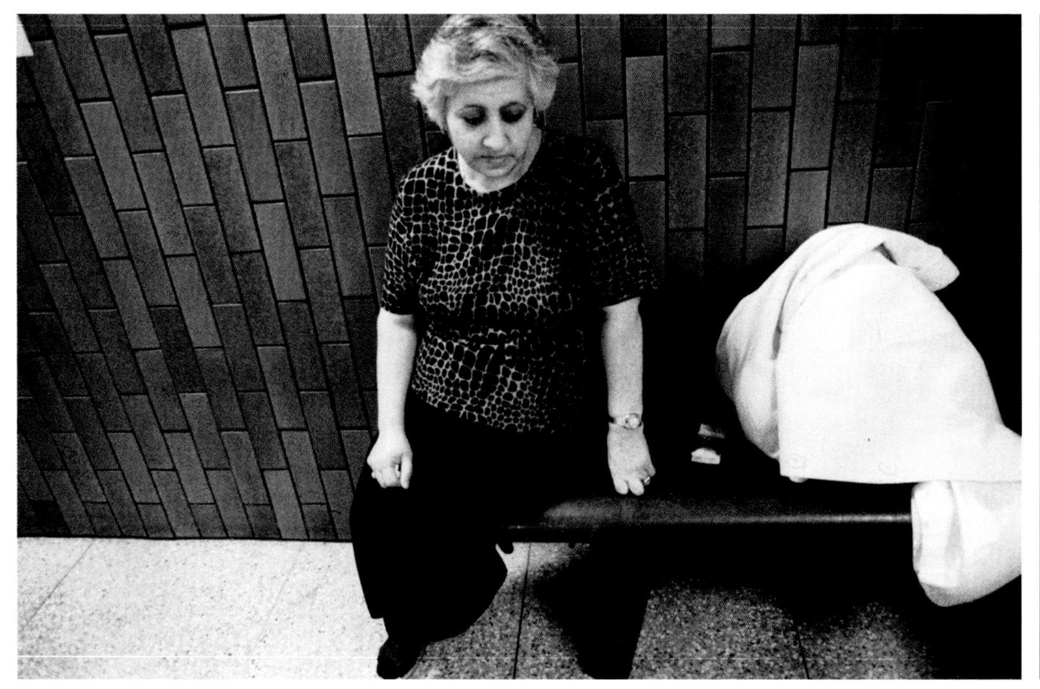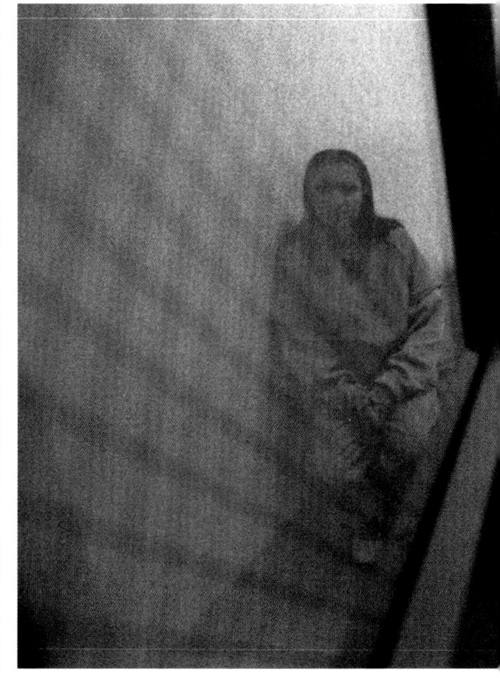

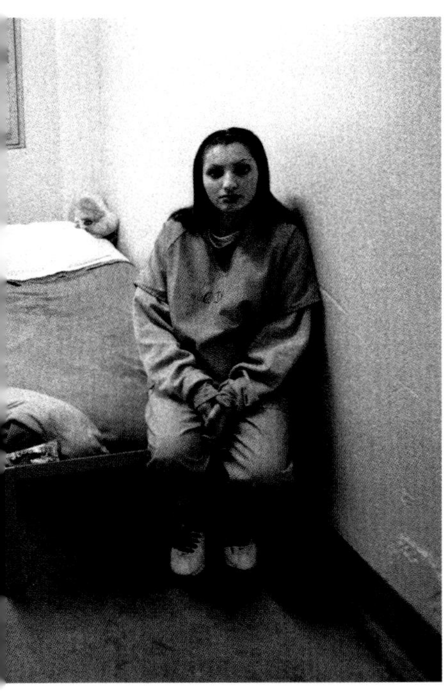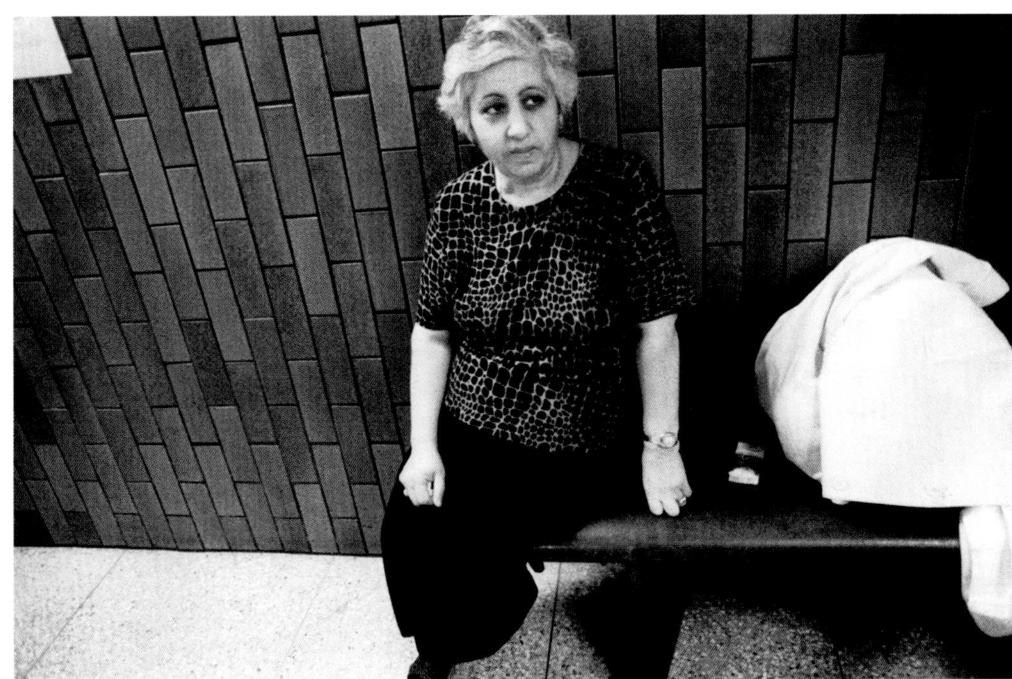

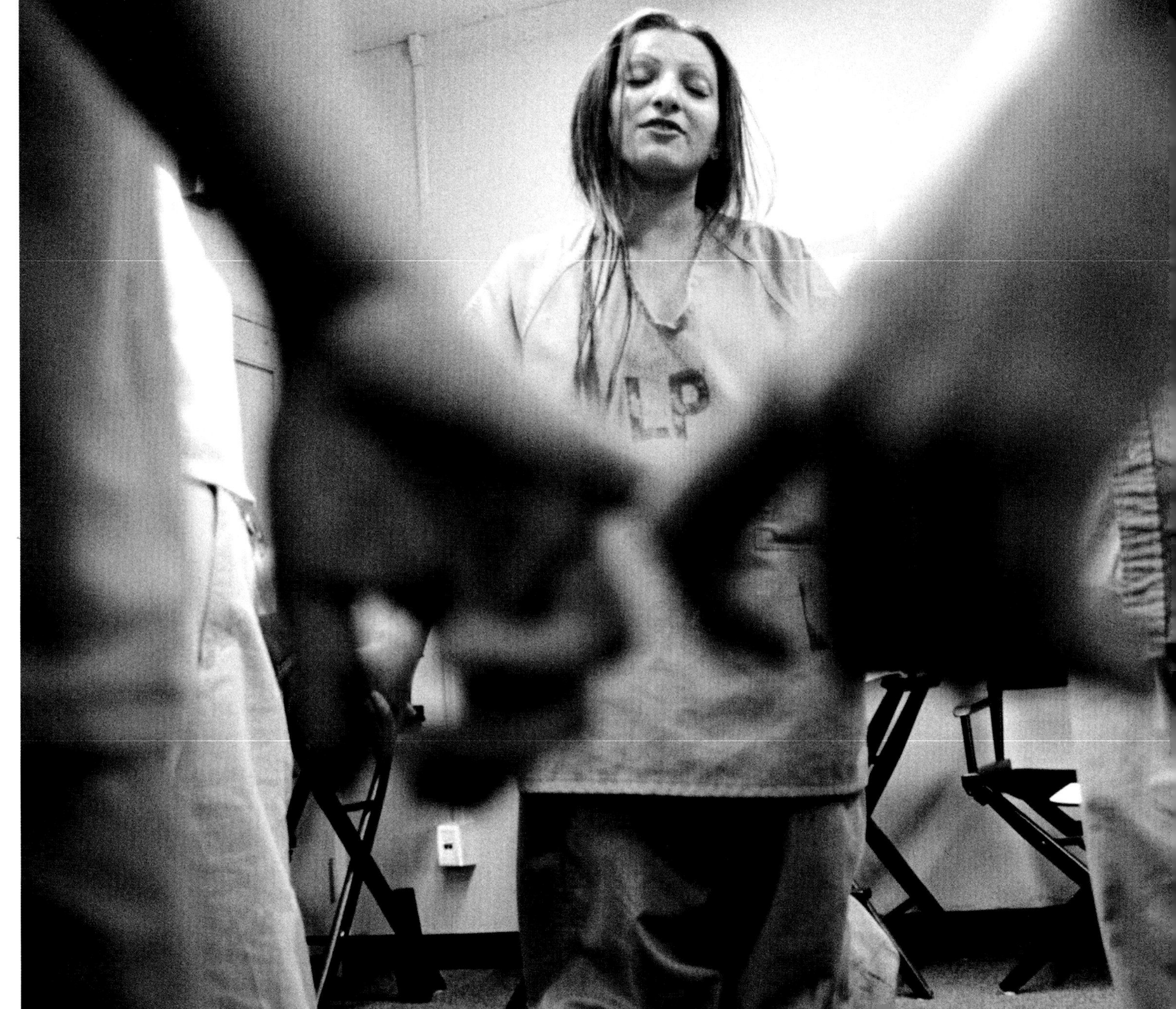

"In school, there was the geeks and stuff and there was the popular group. And I wasn't gonna go hang around with the geeks. So I hung out with the popular people and the popular people were the gang members, of course."

"In school, there was the geeks and stuff and there was the popular group. And I wasn't gonna go hang around with the geeks. So I hung out with the popular people and the popular people were the gang members, of course."

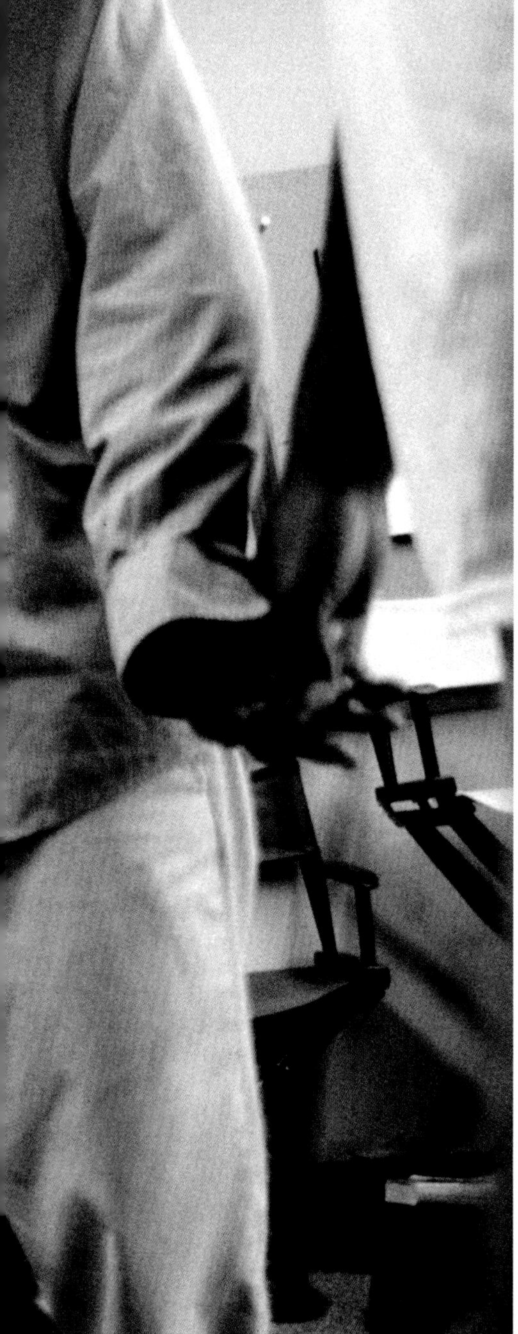

Mayse

EIGHTEEN YEARS OLD

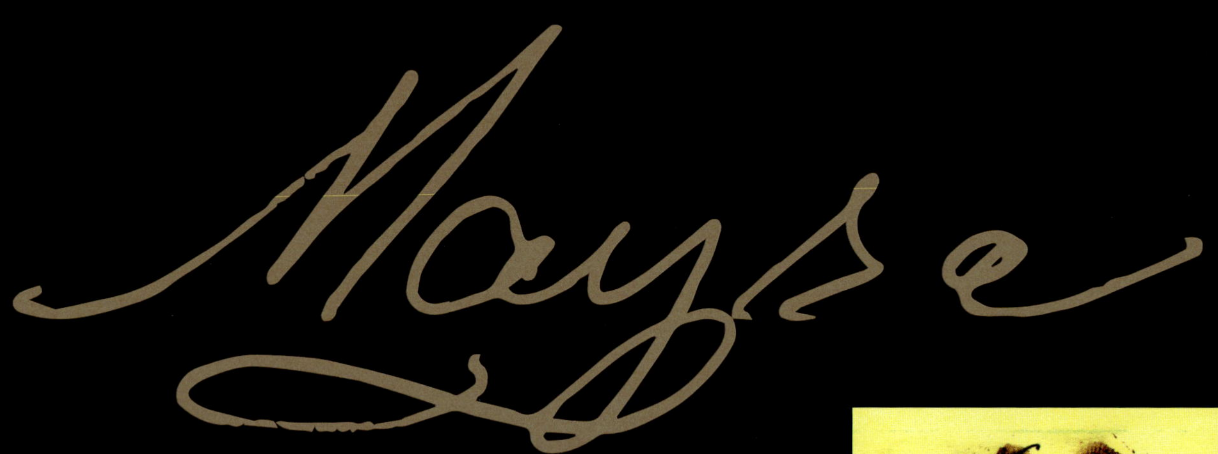

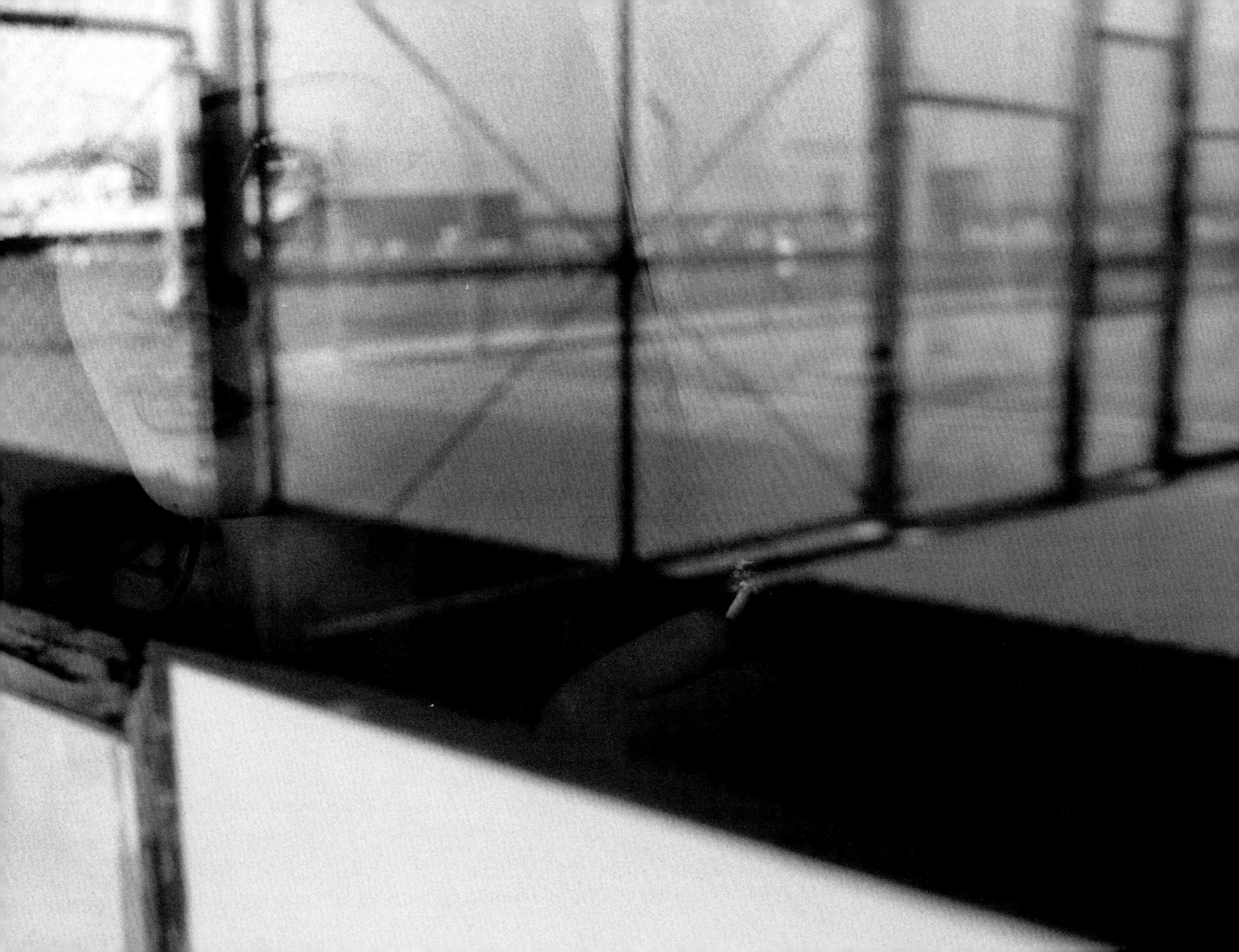

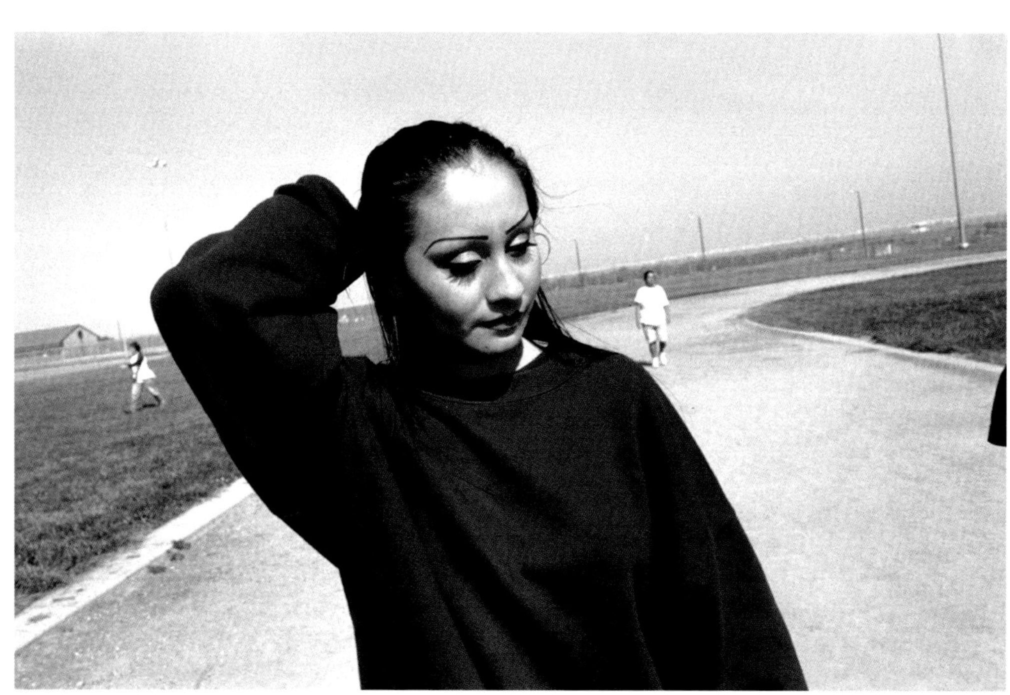

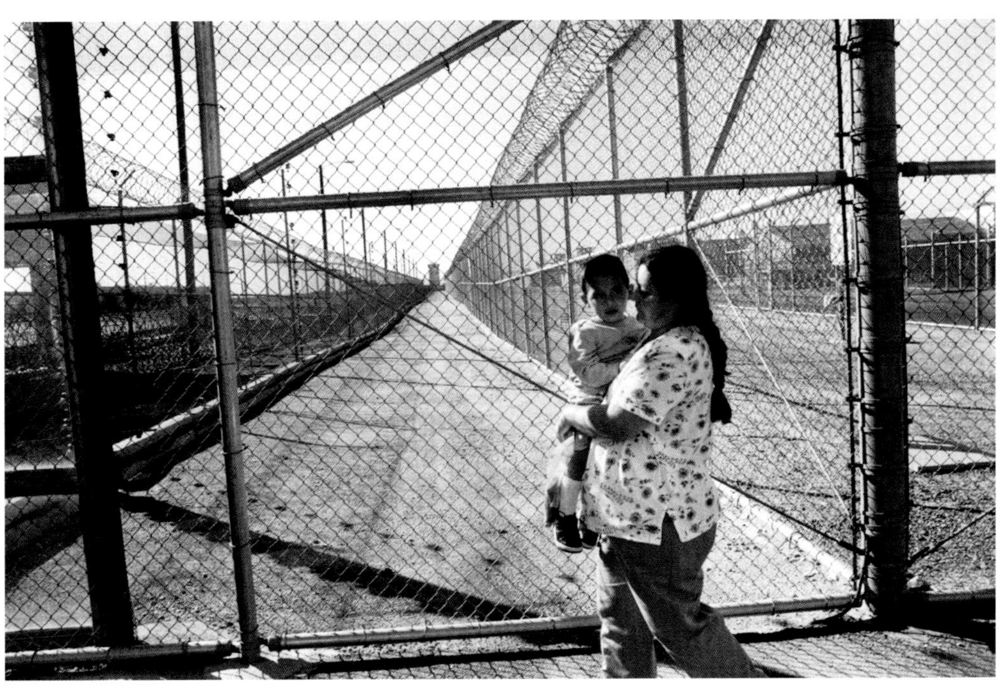

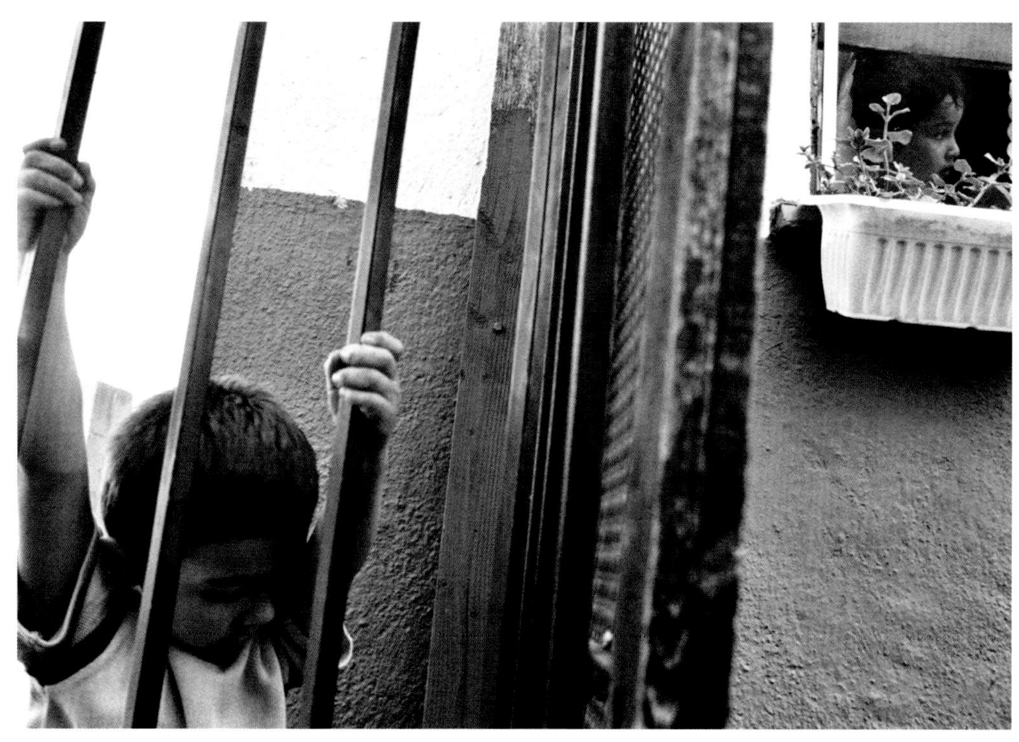

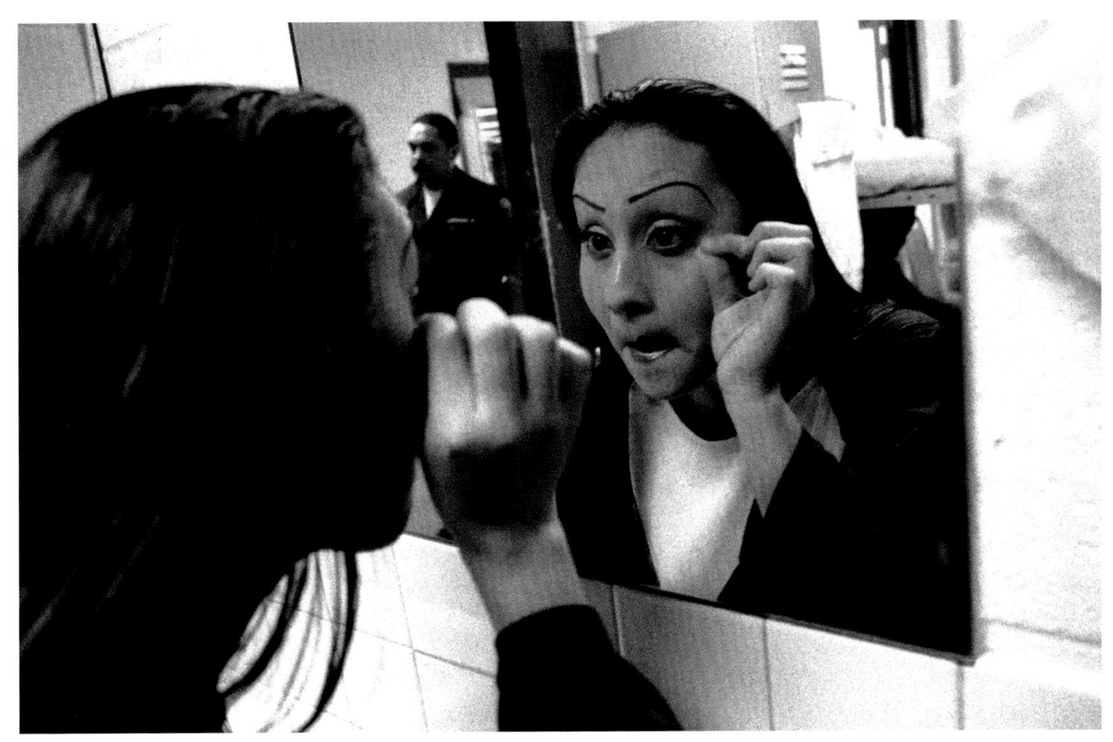

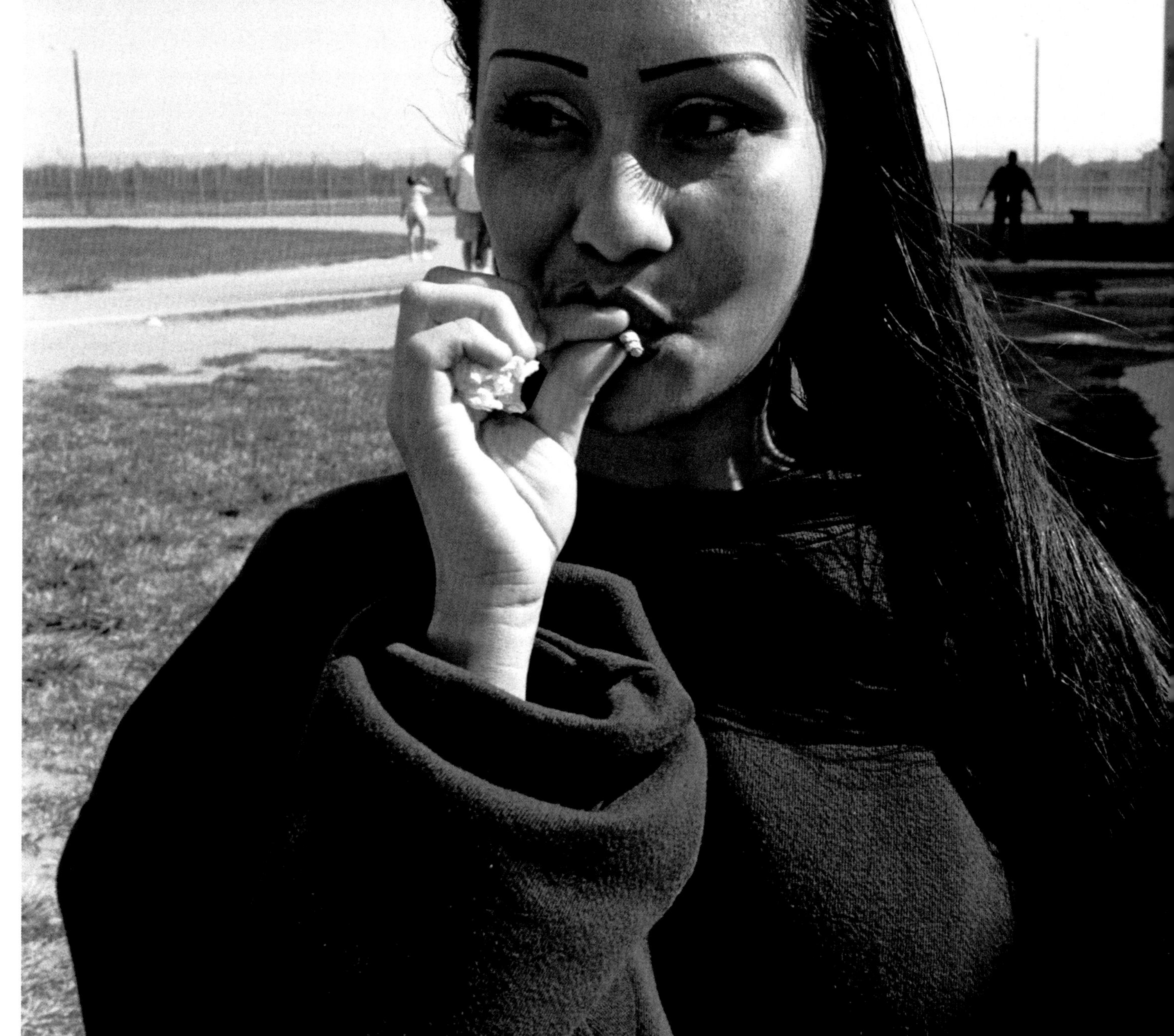

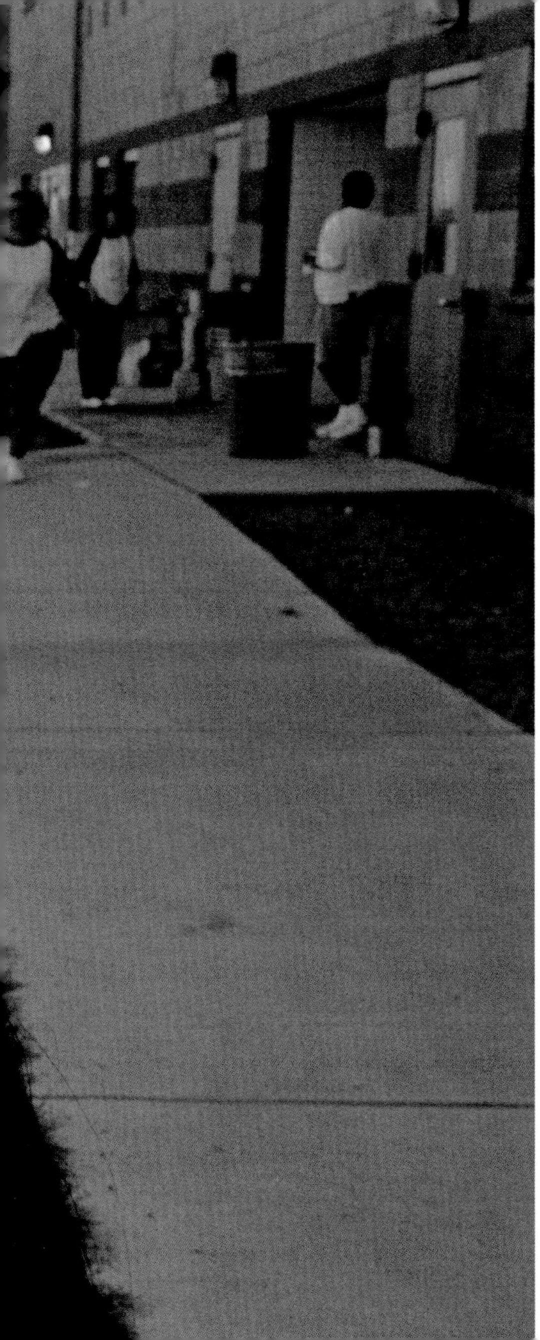

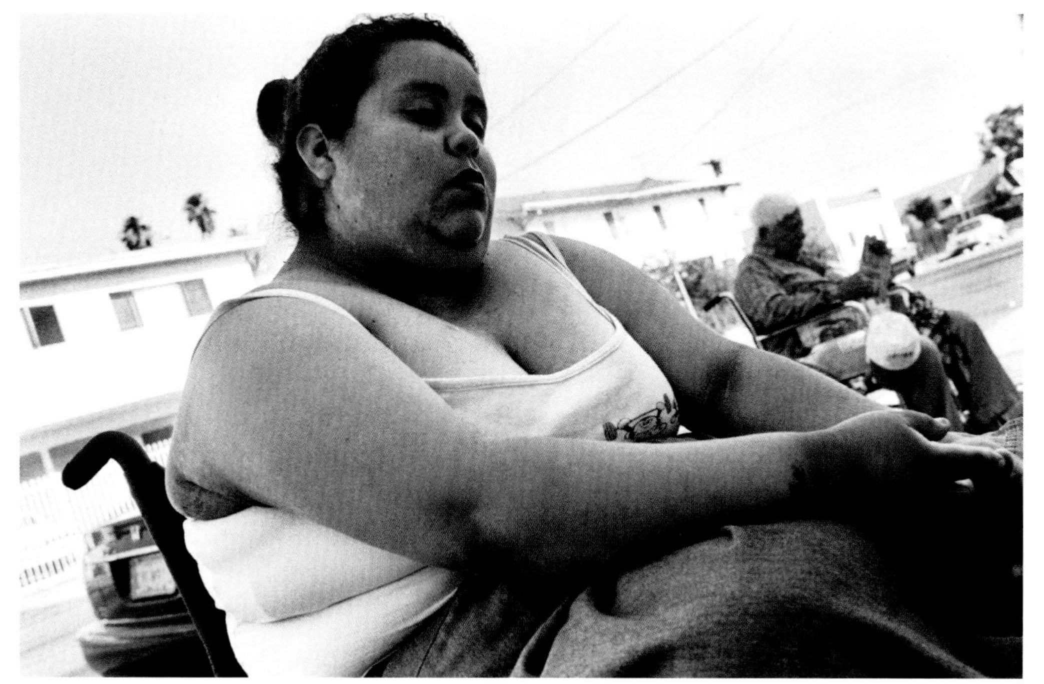
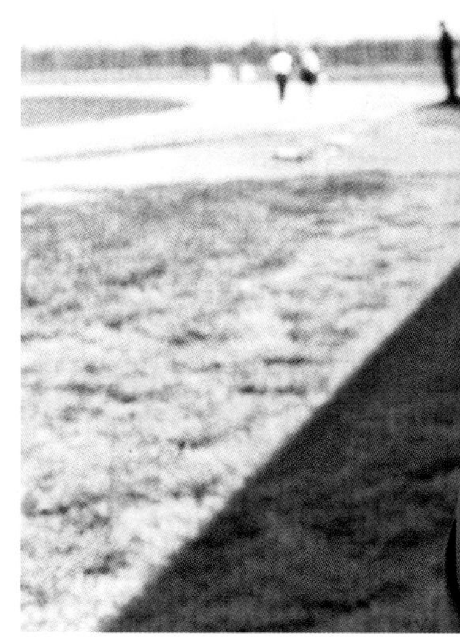

"I was thirteen when I got
involved in gangbanging.
Mayra, she was my road
dog, she was my sister. But
when she was on her drugs,
forget it, she was just a totally
different person. [The shot]
came out of my stomach.
How many shots? I only got
one shot on my stomach and
the other shot ... I still have a
bullet in the back of my head.
That, they cannot take out. I
understand what Mayra went
through, I understand. She
had to do what she had to
do. If she had not done it, the
homeboys would come back
to her or her family. I'm not
mad at her, what happened is
what happened. I still love her
like a sister."

"I was thirteen when I got involved in gangbanging. Mayra, she was my road dog, she was my sister. But when she was on her drugs, forget it, she was just a totally different person. [The shot] came out of my stomach. How many shots? I only got one shot on my stomach and the other shot … I still have a bullet in the back of my head. That, they cannot take out. I understand what Mayra went through, I understand. She had to do what she had to do. If she had not done it, the homeboys would come back to her or her family. I'm not mad at her, what happened is what happened. I still love her like a sister."

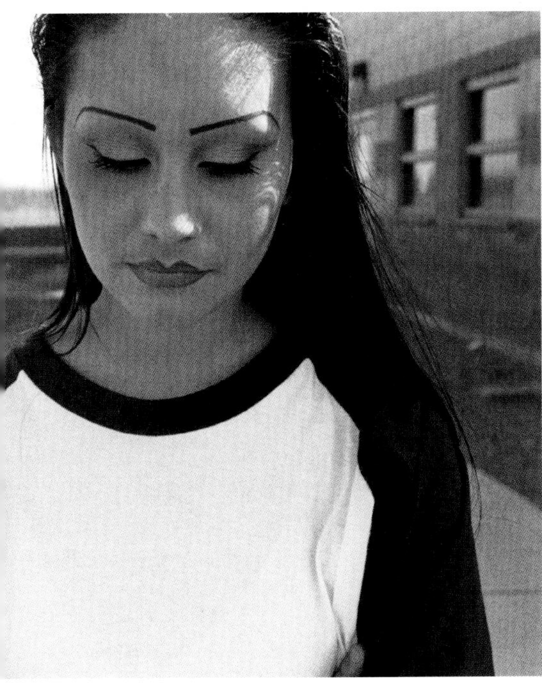
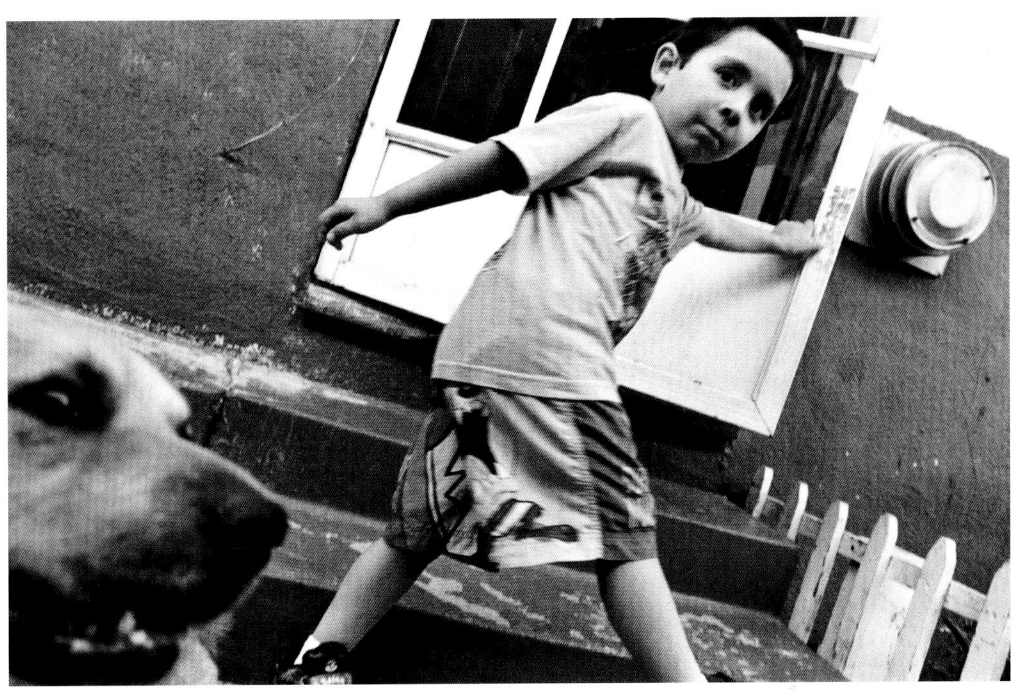

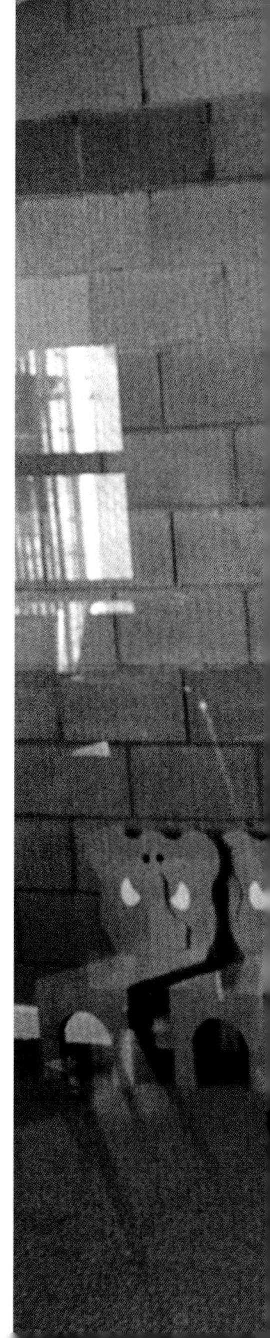

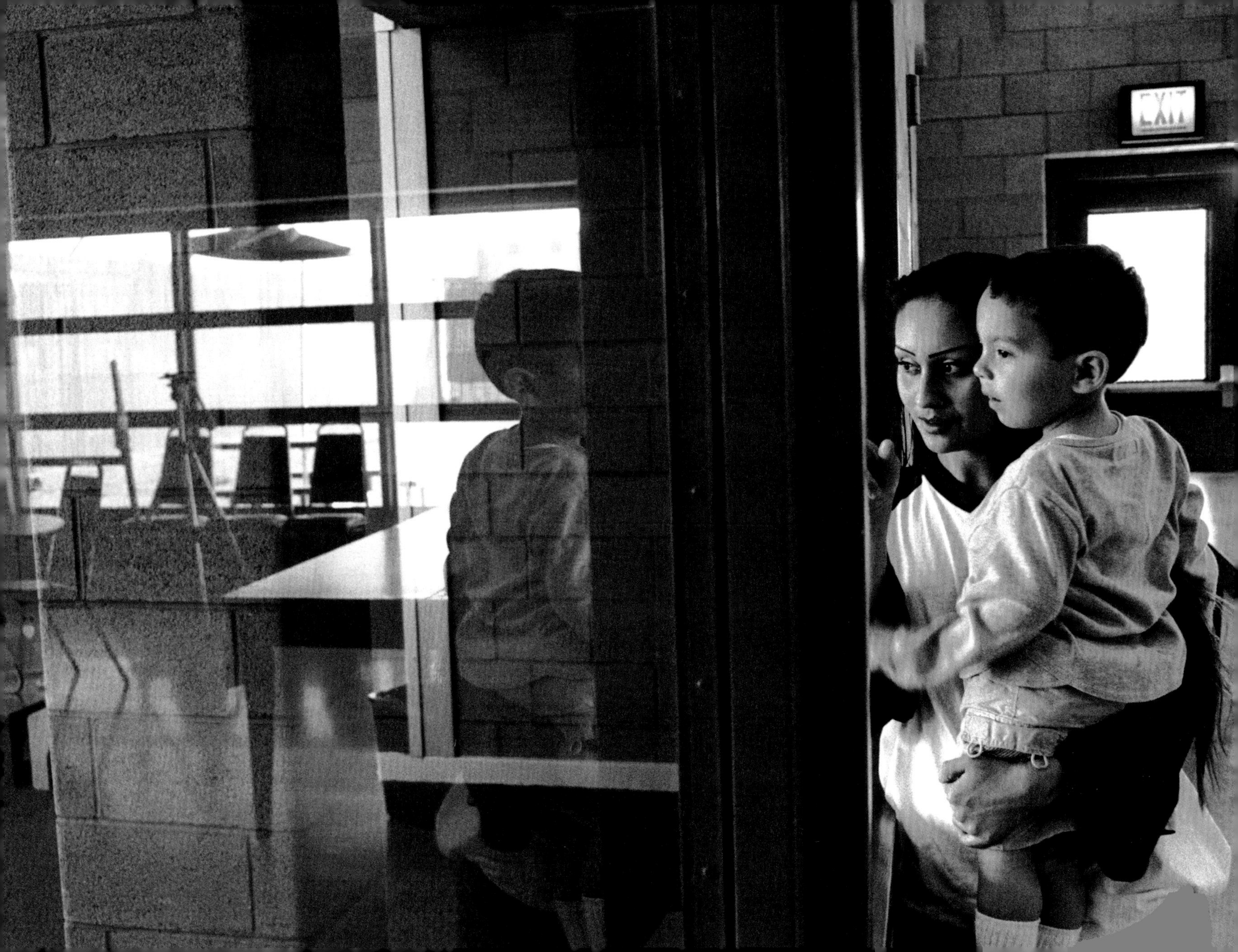

Postscript

by Ara Oshagan

Ara Oshagan is a diasporic transdisciplinary artist, curator, and cultural worker whose practice explores collective and personal histories of marginalization, displacement, identity, legacies of violence, and (un)imagined futures. A descendant of communities uprooted from their indigenous land by the Armenian Genocide, he was born in Beirut, Lebanon, and displaced by war as a youth to the United States. Oshagan has published three books of photography and has exhibited his artwork and public art internationally. He lives in Los Angeles with his family.

I walk swiftly behind Leslie Neale, a filmmaker. We cross through massive metal gates with barbed wire, past tall concrete walls and taciturn guards, and enter into a large, grassy open space. In the distance are low-lying institutional buildings and rows of kids in orange jumpers walking along the concrete pathways. This is Los Angeles Central Juvenile Hall, where Leslie is teaching a film class and making a documentary film about juveniles being tried as adults for having committed violent crimes ranging from first-degree murder to assault with a deadly weapon. Many of these kids, ranging in age from fifteen to twenty, face harsh sentences, including life in prison. She has invited me to photograph with her crew and this is my first time in juvenile hall. I have no idea what to expect. Toughened gang members? Aggressive teenagers with violent attitudes? I brace myself for the trip to the "inside."

We enter a nondescript room with white walls, a window, a table, a few chairs. Leslie has brought an electronic keyboard. The kids walk in one by one. They hide contraband candy under their baggy jumpsuits. They laugh and hassle each other. When I speak to them, they are respectful, deferential even. They are ordinary awkward teenagers. They talk about color balance. Shutter speed. Image thirds. Peter is reading the *Wall Street Journal*, discussing the stock market. He asks me about my work. We talk. We connect immediately. Then he sits down in front of the keyboard and plays Beethoven's "Moonlight Sonata."

I am astounded, floored. I had played the same tune for my son the night before as a lullaby. The barbed wire, the massive walls that I passed by earlier, the metal gates, the guards—everything that separates the inside from the outside—vanish into thin air.

I look at Peter and I can't believe he is incarcerated. I see my young self and my son among this group of kids. And I realize that this project, beyond being about incarceration, is about connection, about breaking down barriers of perception, about a process to humanize these youth against a vast system—internal and external—that incessantly and ruthlessly dehumanizes them. In this book's introduction, Father Greg Boyle speaks of kinship and of the importance of embracing the totality of a person and not the single bad decision they have made. He calls it radical kinship.

For the next three years, we go in and out of LA Central Juvenile Hall, LA County jail and state prisons, visiting the kids in the project.

At sixteen, Peter was arrested for breaking and entering while helping a friend rob a house. We follow him from juvenile hall to county jail as he turns nineteen.

Then to Ironwood State Prison, where he has become buff overnight. He is worried about his father, who has cancer.

We travel to Chowchilla state prison to see Liz—a soft-spoken young woman and a teenage runaway due to sexual abuse as a child—who writes long letters and poetry. Liz was arrested at the age of fifteen for being a witness to a murder. She was sentenced to eleven years.

And Sandra, who grew up without parents and was a victim of rape at twelve years of age. At seventeen, she was arrested and charged for accessory to murder; a phone card with her name was found at the scene of a crime. She was sentenced to twenty-seven years to life. She is a devout Christian, struggling with her faith.

And Tehachapi to see Duc, a smart young man and a victim of domestic physical abuse. He was sentenced to thirty-five years to life even though he only drove the getaway car from a crime scene. A gun was fired from the back seat of the car he was driving. No one was hurt in the incident.

And Anait, who at fourteen would become, at the time, the youngest person to be tried as an adult in California. She, too, was only a driver to the scene of a crime. She got seven years.

All of their crimes were their first offense.

Facing abuse, neglect, and marginalization while growing up, these kids made bad decisions when they hardly knew how to make a decision. They have so much potential to bring beauty and goodness to our world. Why are they being put away for years, decades?

I worked on this project from 2000 to 2003, then put it aside. It evolved in my mind and my imagination for many years.

In the two decades since I took these photographs, little has changed in the US prison-industrial complex. Prison spaces and mass incarceration look the same today as they did then. Incarceration rates, for youth and adults, have dropped but are still astronomically high. The United States still leads the world in per capita incarceration rates. A system overwhelmingly geared towards dehumanization and punishment has a nearly 75% recidivism rate. Juvenile halls and prisons remain overcrowded and offer little rehabilitation. They are often dangerous, especially for youth, and provide substandard health and mental-health care. If anything, the situation has deteriorated. In 2023, for example, California state regulators shut down LA Central Juvenile Hall, citing "unsuitable" and "inhumane" conditions for youth incarcerated there. The prison-industrial complex has adjusted slightly, yet it has not changed in any fundamental way.

On a brisk morning in 2023, I walk into a coffee shop in Los Angeles and stare at Peter. He stands. He smiles. We hug and laugh in disbelief. Last time I saw him was in Ironwood State Prison more than twenty years ago. We have exchanged dozens of letters over the years. At some point, we lost touch. But while preparing this book, I searched for him, and incredibly, we were able to reconnect.

I am incredulous. We have come full circle. Peter is married with five-year-old twins. He has a business. He works long hours. He is uplifted and happy. He tells me that the tough life he has lived has made him who he is today. His time in prison is part of who he is—he fully embraces it. He laughs. He is happy. "Life is good," he says. "Life is good. I am who I am."

I tell him he is astounding. I feel a closeness, a bond, lasting over decades, stretching into the future. I feel I am standing in kinship.

Peter

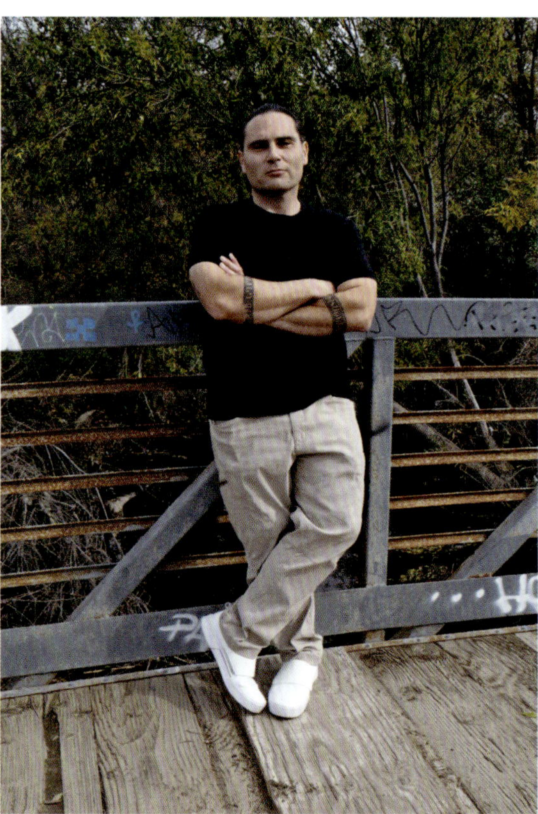

Peter, Los Angeles, 2023.

Life is good. Life is good. Yeah, life is good, man.

I did ten years in prison. I have been out for twelve.

I'm really happy today. Really. I have a family, a wife. I have two unbelievable kids. They're thriving. They're thriving. My kids are something else. The most well-mannered, smartest, happiest, spoiled, blessed kids I know. They're just something else. They blow my mind every time they open their mouths, they blow my mind. And it's kind of a reality check sometimes when you see yourself in them. It shapes the way you are. Yeah, it's a blessing. My wife—the greatest, greatest mother. Better than my mother. Better than her mother. I don't know. The universe put her in my path, I think, for a reason. She knows the person I am. My mission in life is my family. And not just my wife and kids, but my brother too. Staying close to my people. My clan, my blood. And it's working out. It's working out. I'm happy. I'm really happy, actually. I can't describe in words how I feel about life. I'm very, very, very fortunate.

I mean, I got locked up when I was a kid, seventeen years old, a kid. It was scary. It was life-changing. It's like getting thrown into the ocean off the pier and then the pier disappears, and you don't know what is happening, what direction to go. It's a shock. You panic. And then you kind of adapt. You get used to it, almost. It becomes your everyday, becomes your life.

At first, you become more religious because you're looking for some-thing—a floating device, a lifeline, something. Yeah. I got into the faith, started reading the Bible. That kind of developed my mentality into being a good person, a decent person, not an asshole. Even though you're surrounded by assholes. I don't know. I understood from when I was young that there's a right way, there's a wrong way. And yeah, you could do some things wrong sometimes. Not every-body can follow that straight path all the time. You stray once in a while. But you either become a better or worse person because of it. Fortunately, I was the type that became a better person. It was just in the stars.

The first year I got out was really a tough time. You're just thrown into reality, everything is coming at you, like, fast, live. You have no outside life experience, no work experience, no trades, no skills. Yeah, maybe you picked something up in prison. But outside everything is brand-new and it's coming at you fast. Things you thought about for years ... you get out and you realize, that's not the way it was [laughs]! In prison, everything is high. The ceilings are fifteen, twenty,

twenty-five feet high. The buildings all have two or three tiers. You're either outside or you're in, like, an airplane hangar. Everything's open. Even your cell ceiling is a little higher. Well, I remember my first impression when I got home, when I first walked into our apartment—I was like, holy shit, it feels cramped. Like a giant walked into a little house. You know, I'm not that big of a person, but it just felt enclosed. I left the cage and home felt like a different cage.

Inside, you kind of knew who the snakes were, you know, the people you should stay away from. The good people in there guided you. Hey, do this, don't do that. It's a different world, a different jungle. It has its own rules. A lot of camaraderie, a lot of discipline. The daily regimen teaches you to be focused and disciplined. There's a definite brotherhood. Like soldiers in war.

It's all based on respect. If you leave something in the middle of the table and you came back a week later, it would be in the exact same place. Nobody would touch it. Stealing is a big no-no in there. There is a different code, a different ethic in prison than out here. Out here, everybody's just out for themselves. They're just cut-throat. They wake up every morning thinking, How can I get ahead? You meet someone, you don't know who he is, what he's about, what he's going to do, what does he want?

It was a lot easier in the joint than it is out here in every respect, in every respect except having the freedom to see your family, friends, go here, go there. That had to be the hardest part of it. Yeah. Not being able to do what you wanted to do. But then again, you don't have the freedom out here, either, to do whatever you want. You have to do whatever you can.

I have good friends from prison. We go fishing, hunting, shooting. They dogsit for me. My celly [cellmate] for two years got out before me. And without me asking, bought a bouquet of roses for my mom, for Mother's Day. Just out of the blue. Hey, this is from Pete, he told her. It's tough to find somebody out here that would do that for you. And these friends, I can call them at 3 a.m. and tell them, Hey, wake up, I need you. They're there. No questions asked. They'll drop everything and run. I miss that camaraderie. I miss that discipline and brotherhood.

Regrets? No, not at all. At all. I strongly believe the person I am today was shaped by everything that happened in my past. Everything from the positive to the negative. If you're a good person today, if you like the person that you are, then you just have to embrace everything that happened in your past. Because if something was different, you might not be the person that you are. If I didn't get locked up, who knows? Maybe, maybe I would have been an addict or I would have been a thief or I would have been a rapist. Who knows? Who knows? That's kind of the mentality I've had for a long time. Everything that happened in the past, you have to embrace it.

So, no, no regrets. I regret that I was away from my family. That I didn't get to experience some of the things that maybe my peers experienced. But they didn't get to experience some of the things I experienced. And I don't know … I like me, I like me. You know, it's not an egotistical thing. I'm not being braggadocious. I just like the person that I am because I know I'm a good person. And if I hadn't gone to prison, none of this other stuff would be in my life. I wouldn't have this family, these kids, these friends. I wouldn't have this mindset, outlook, appreciation of life.

I wouldn't have this knowledge. Prison teaches you a lot about life.

I wouldn't change anything. I'd do it all over again. Exactly the same. Exactly the same way.

Life is good [*laughs*], life is good. My life is good. I have no complaints. No qualms. No weight on my shoulders. No "I should have done this, I should have done that." It is what it is, man. It is what it is …

––––––––––––––––––––––

From an interview with Peter by Ara Oshagan, December 2023.

Captions

Acknowledgments

Deep gratitude to Peter, Liz, Duc, Sandra, Efrain, Anait, Mayra, and Nancy and their families for letting me into their lives and trusting me with their stories. As well to the many incarcerated individuals and corrections officers and staff that I met and photographed during this project.

I am singularly indebted to Leslie Neale and Change Films for taking a chance with me and allowing me to be part of their film crew to photograph. Without Leslie and her incredible access to Central Juvenile Hall, Los Angeles County Jail, and state prisons, this book would not have been possible.

Special thanks to Father Gregory Boyle for a wonderful and insightful foreword. He has taught me the power of radical kinship.

Gratitude to Nubar Alexanian for photo editing early on in this project, Viken Berberian for quick-fire and surgical text editing and feedback, Joseph Rodriguez for guidance, and Pete Brook for insight.

Special thanks to my friend and brother, Peter, for telling his story with such honesty.

This book is for Anahid, Sebouh, Adom, Shahan, and Aren: always and always.